Woven Into Prayer

Angela Ashwin is the compiler of the bestselling *The Book of a Thousand Prayers* and *A Little Book of Healing Prayer* (both HarperCollins) and author of the recently published *Faith in the Fool* (DLT). Greatly in demand as a speaker and retreat leader, she lives in Southwell and is a Lay Canon.

Publications by the same author include:

Heaven in Ordinary
The Book of a Thousand Prayers
The Wine Danced
Faith in the Fool
Wait and See (CD Rom)

Woven Into Prayer

*A flexible pattern of daily prayer
through the Christian year*

Angela Ashwin

CANTERBURY
PRESS

Norwich

First published in 1999 by The Canterbury Press
Norwich (a publishing imprint of Hymns Ancient &
Modern Limited, a registered charity)
13A Hellesdon Park Road,
Norwich NR6 5DR

New edition 2010

British Library Cataloguing in Publication Data

A catalogue record for this book is available
from the British Library

ISBN 978-1-84825-052-9

Typeset by Regent Typesetting, London
Printed in Great Britain by CPI Bookmarque,
Croydon CR0 4TD

For friends and fellow-worshippers at
Southwell Minster

Contents

Contents

Contents

Preface

Books like this grow out of corporate experience, and this new edition of *Woven into Prayer* is no exception. I owe a great deal to the insights of friends and colleagues who follow various patterns of daily prayer, and to some helpful feedback from users of the first edition. I am also grateful to my editor, Christine Smith, for encouraging me to continue exploring the vision of praying through the Christian year. Sister Margaret Tournour RSCJ, who put so much into the seasonal illustrations, sadly died in 2003; her contributions, like those of the other artist, Paul Judson, add incomparably to the book.

A few errors have been corrected, one season has a new name, and there is a fresh Introduction. Other than that it is the same book.

Southwell, Notts, 2010.

Introduction

Prayer and faith are anything but dead. In spite of the best efforts of some people to convince us that nobody bothers very much with God these days, the truth is that countless men and women continue to pray in countless different ways. A prime example of this is the increasing number of Christians who use an order of daily prayer, because they find that this regular engagement with Scripture and seasonal imagery anchors them in God and feeds their inner life. Where *Woven into Prayer* differs from similar books is that I have made the daily prayer pattern as flexible as possible, to offset the perpetual sense of guilt that can easily beset busy people. Even if you want to pray with a Daily Office (or 'set form of prayer'), your circumstances and lifestyle may make this so difficult that you end up discouraged and tempted to give up altogether. I have therefore included only one order of prayer for each day (rather than a 'morning and evening' structure), and have designed the material so that it will expand or contract according to how busy you are that day. My hope is that this will deepen your relationship with God rather than becoming just one more burden. But this book is not only for hard-pressed people, and there is also a section under each season entitled *A Quiet Space*, for those who want something more than just a Daily Office. Suggestions here include ideas for praying with silence, icons, imaginative reflections and *Lectio Divina* ('Sacred Reading').

Not long after the first edition of this book came out, one reader I encountered was rather concerned that I had allowed for such flexibility within the discipline of prayer. I can understand the anxiety that I might seem to be encouraging a casual or half-hearted approach to the spiritual life. When we pray it is good to remember that we are opening ourselves up to the living God whose love is like a refining fire. This God knows us utterly and is waiting to mend, heal and transform us into the persons we were created to be. If we are ruthlessly honest with ourselves, we will know if we are allowing our commitment to slip. That is quite different from those times when life is so demanding that we simply cannot cope with any form of prayer that is too long or complicated. The good news is that God knows this too, and will not wave a big stick at us when the pressure is high or our energy-level low. Since the quality of our prayer is not measured by the number of words we use (cf. Matthew 6:7) but by the depth of our openness and surrender to God, we can take heart and allow whatever words and concepts we have encountered to penetrate us and do their work. Prayer is as much what God is doing as what we are doing.

Over the last ten years there has been an increasing awareness of the rhythm of the Christian year, with its rich tapestry of themes and images. Our journey through the cycle of the church's seasons goes back to the earliest centuries and contains two distinct sections, with weeks of 'Ordinary Time' between them. The first part takes us from All Saints' Tide (starting on All Saints' Day, 1 November), through the expectancy of Advent, and into the celebration of Christ's birth and Epiphany (literally the 'revealing') of his glory. The season of Epiphany ends on 2 February with the feast of the Presentation of the Child Jesus in the Temple, also known as Candlemas. Light is a major theme on this day because it is when the old man Simeon recognized that Jesus is 'a light to enlighten the Gentiles' (Luke 2:32a). This is followed by the first period of Ordinary Time in the year, during which we rest from the drama and colourful motifs of the major seasons and rediscover God in the ordinariness of life. On Ash Wednesday we pick up the second major sequence in the liturgical year. Now we journey with Jesus through the wilderness days of Lent and into his passion and death in Holy Week, followed by the celebrations of Easter, the Ascension and the gift of the Holy Spirit at Pentecost. I have begun this book with Advent because it is the traditional start of the church's year. But the transition from the mid-year period of Ordinary Time 2 into All Saints' Tide still marks an important shift, as we remind ourselves of our connectedness with the whole communion of saints in those special days before Advent. I have also delineated a five-week period after Pentecost, in order to provide more time specifically to ponder the impact and significance of the Holy Spirit on our lives.

The Christian year does not only connect us with key aspects of the story of Jesus. It also reflects fundamental human experiences of darkness and waiting, and the movement from pain and failure into healing, hope and trust. There are obvious parallels here with the natural order of the seasons, although the calendar of the church's year is like a spiral, taking us ever deeper into God, rather than a never-ending cycle from death to life experienced in the same way each year. For example, spring flowers, lambs and chicks will all die, but nothing can destroy the risen Jesus or the love which has proved stronger than everything the powers of evil can throw at him[1].

There may also be times when we do not feel particularly joyful at Christmas and Easter, or when all our prayer feels dull or uninspired. We may even find ourselves hanging on by a thread to the classic Christian themes of forgiveness and renewal, with our sense of God's presence virtually gone. If that is the case, we are not letting God down or becoming weak disciples. On the contrary, you could say that our prayer is of extra value at such times, because we are persevering in pure, blind faith when there is apparently very little in it for us. We have no idea what effect our praying is having, either inside us or in the world around us, and God may well be working in ways we could not possibly imagine. The main thing is that we remain faithful. There are times when it is best to allow ourselves simply to be carried by the liturgy, leaning on the symbols and affirmations in which we *want* to believe, and trusting that our efforts to pray will be received with infinite tenderness by the Divine Lover whose initiative and desire for us lie behind the whole story of salvation.

While every season has its own mood and flavour, each one flows into the next and there are no rigid divisions between them. Our longing for the coming of Christ into our world is not restricted to Advent, any more than we stop celebrating the resurrection after Eastertide. But to be taken up into the Christian story, especially as reflected in the church's year, is to come face to face with themes and symbols that have the potential to challenge and enrich our relationship with God, if we allow each season to ask us its own particular questions.

The shape of the book

Material for each day consists of:

- *A Thread for the Day:* a verse or short passage from Scripture
- *A Short Order of Daily Prayer:* a simple piece of liturgy

- *A Quiet Space:* suggestions for reflective, imaginative and other kinds of prayer, which could take anything from fifteen to thirty minutes
- *Night-Time Blessing:* to close the day

You may be able to pray with all these elements in a day. But if life is hectic you might only manage the *Thread for the Day,* taking this with you as a kind of travelling companion. Even on the busiest of days, there will generally be a few opportunities to recall that particular verse or phrase and realign yourself with God's love. Another possibility is to have a *Quiet Space* with God at the start of the day and to use the *Order of Daily Prayer* later. Follow whatever pattern makes sense for you.

The *Short Order of Daily Prayer* follows a traditional outline:

Opening sentences

Psalm

Bible Reading

Canticle (literally 'little song'; most of these come from the Bible but are not in the Psalms)

Prayers (if you would like to use special prayers for Saints' Days and other major feasts these can be found in Appendix A on page 255)

Conclusion

In a set form of prayer like this there is always a danger that we feel the need to 'get through' it. Certainly we are 'going with the flow' of the words, making the Office into an offering to God as we do so. But to rattle through the text with one eye on the clock is obviously a nonsense. That is why I have suggested a pause at the beginning of the prayers and after the Bible reading, to help us gather our thoughts and reflect quietly on what we have read. If there are interruptions, or if time runs out, I find it best simply to let the order of prayer go, without stress, and to finish with the closing couplet. Hopefully whatever time we have been given, whether short or long, will give us a stronger sense of walking with God through the rest of the day.

Some practical points

In each *Short Order of Daily Prayer*, two psalms and two Bible passages are printed out in full, so that you can, if you wish, use the book anywhere without having to carry a Bible as well. But there are also lists of suggested daily Bible readings and of other appropriate psalms at the back of the book, to provide variety and a continuous flow of Scripture through the year. I have left a gap on Sundays in this lectionary, to allow a day to catch up if needed, or else to leave space for you to absorb the readings that are being used in church that day. *Woven into Prayer* is designed primarily for individual use, so the first person singular is used more often than the plural form. But the prayers could also be prayed in a group by taking the verses alternately. The text could be adapted by saying, for example, 'Lord, touch our lips,' instead of 'my lips.' If you are feeling adventurous you could also sing some of the psalms and canticles, either with traditional chant or your own melodies.

Introduction

Part of Something Bigger

We are never alone when we pray because we are part of the wider fellowship of Christian people, supporting each other as fellow-members of the Body of Christ. Through the mystery of our inter-connectedness our small offering of prayer is taken up into the ceaseless worship of the 'great cloud of witnesses' in heaven and on earth (cf. Hebrews 12:1a, Revelation 4: 9–11, 7: 9–12). The psalms in particular link us with the continuous stream of prayer that goes back to Jesus himself, and beyond that to the people of the Old Testament. There is always a bond between people who pray, and I hope that those who use this book will feel encouraged by the fact that they are united with others who are weaving a similar thread of prayer into their lives.

'Behold I make all things new' (from Revelation 21: 5)

Prayer is always a new beginning, not in the depressing sense of perpetually going back to square one, but because there is a freshness every time we turn once more to God. Each moment of prayer is full of forgiveness and hope because of the potential of what God will do with us and in us. Whenever we pray we are remade and renewed. In spite of ourselves, we find that our lives and our very selves are being, gradually and imperceptibly, woven into prayer. That is pure gift.

7

Advent

ADVENT

Advent Sunday to Christmas Eve

The name 'Advent' comes from the Latin for 'coming' or 'arrival'. During this season we look forward to Christ's coming among us, and we ponder the great mysteries of the ultimate summing up of all things in him, beyond time.

A THREAD FOR THE DAY

Sunday

A voice cries out, 'In the wilderness prepare the way of the Lord! Make straight in the desert a highway for our God.' Then the glory of the Lord shall be revealed, and all people shall see it together, for the mouth of the Lord has spoken it. Get you up to a high mountain, O herald of good tidings, and say to the cities of Judah, 'Behold, your God!'

Isaiah 40: 3, 5, 9

Monday

Rejoice and exult with all your heart, O daughter of Jerusalem! The Lord has taken away the judgements against you, he has cast out your enemies. The King of Israel, the Lord, is in your midst; you shall fear evil no more. He will rejoice over you with gladness, and dance with you in his love.

Zephaniah 3: 14b–15, 17b

Tuesday

Truly my soul waits in stillness upon God; my salvation comes from him.

Psalm 62: 1

Wednesday

St Paul writes, 'Marana tha! Our Lord, come! The grace of the Lord Jesus be with you. My love be with you all in Christ Jesus. Amen.'

1 Corinthians 16: 22b–4

Thursday

You know what hour it is, how it is now the moment for you to wake from sleep. For salvation is nearer to us now than when we first believed.

Romans 13: 11

Friday

Put on the whole armour of light, and cast off the works of darkness. Now is the time to keep alert and to pray always in the power of the Spirit.

Paraphrase of Ephesians 6: 11, 18

Saturday

See what love the Father has given us, that we should be called children of God; and that is what we are. It does not yet appear what we shall be, but we know that when he appears we shall be like him, for we shall see him as he is.

1 John 3: 1a, 2

A SHORT ORDER OF DAILY PRAYER

A moment of quiet: be still and know that God is here.

Begin with today's short piece of Scripture, under A Thread for the Day, and reflect on that for a moment.

Lord, touch my lips:
 that I may sing your praise with all my heart.

Lord, come quickly, come to my aid:
 awaken me to your presence.

Glory to God, Father, Son and Holy Spirit:
 mystery of love, behind, through and beyond all things.

In quietness and trust my soul waits for you:
 Amen and amen! Come, Lord Jesus!

As I turn my face to you, O God,
let my worship be once more a new beginning:
cleanse my spirit in your mercy,
draw me ever deeper into your love,
and accept my offering of praise and prayer
on behalf of the world;
through Jesus Christ,
our Brother and our Saviour. Amen.

Advent

From 17 to 23 December, you could say one of the Great Os of Advent at this point (see pages 19–20).

Psalm 62

1 For God alone my soul waits in silence:
  from him comes my salvation.

2 He only is my rock and my salvation:
  my stronghold, so that I shall not be shaken.

3 How long will you plot against someone to destroy him:
  as though he were a leaning wall or a tottering fence?

4 Their plan is to bring him down, and their delight is in lies:
  they bless with their lips but curse in their hearts.

5 For God alone my soul waits in silence:
  for my hope is in him.

6 He only is my rock and my salvation:
  my stronghold so that I shall not be shaken.

7 On God rests my deliverance and my honour:
  he is my strong rock and my shelter.

8 Put your trust in him always, O people:
  pour out your hearts before him, for God is our refuge.

9 Put no trust in extortion:
  if riches increase, set not your heart on them.

10 God has spoken once; twice have I heard him say:
    that power belongs to him.

11 Steadfast love belongs to you, O Lord:
    you will repay us all according to our deeds.

> *God our rock,*
> *help us to put our trust in you;*
> *show us where our true security lies,*
> *and keep us faithful*
> *as we wait for the coming of your Son,*
> *Jesus Christ, our Saviour. Amen.*

OR

Psalm 130

1 Out of the depths have I called to you, O Lord:
    Lord, hear my voice.

2 O let your ears consider well:
    the voice of my supplication.

3 If you, O Lord, should note what is done amiss:
    who then, Lord, could stand?

4 But there is forgiveness with you:
    therefore you shall be feared.

5 I wait for the Lord, my soul waits for him:
    in his word is my hope.

6 My soul waits for the Lord,
    more than the night-watch for the morning:
    more, I say, than the night-watch for the morning.

7 O Israel, trust in the Lord:
 for with him there is steadfast love,
  and plenteous redemption.

8 And he will redeem Israel:
 from all their sins.

 Merciful God, I reach out to you
 from the depths of my heart,
 and await with eagerness
 the dawning of your light in the world
 in the coming of Jesus Christ,
 your Son our Lord. Amen.

Other psalms suitable for **Advent** are numbers 33, 42, 50, 70, 72, 75, 76, 80, 94.

Or you may want to use a psalm with a particular theme, see pages 235–237.

At the end of the psalm you could use one of the psalm prayers above, or the Gloria:

Glory to the Father, and to the Son:
 and to the Holy Spirit;
as it was in the beginning, is now:
 and shall be for ever. Amen.

SCRIPTURE READING

Be dressed for action and have your lamps lit; be like those who are waiting for their master to return from the wedding banquet, so that they may open the door for him as soon as he comes and knocks. Blessed are those servants whom the master finds alert when he comes; truly I tell you, he will fasten his belt and have them sit down to eat, and he will come and serve them. If he comes during the middle of the night, or near dawn, and finds them so, blessed are those servants! But know this: if the owner of the house had known at what hour the thief was coming, he would not have let his house be broken into. You also must be ready, for the Son of man is coming at an unexpected hour.

Luke 12: 35–40

OR

The wilderness and the dry land shall be glad, the desert shall rejoice and blossom; like the crocus it shall blossom abundantly, and rejoice with joy and singing. The glory of Lebanon shall be given to it, the majesty of Carmel and Sharon. They shall see the glory of the Lord, the majesty of our God.

Strengthen the weak hands, and make firm the feeble knees. Say to those who are of a fearful heart, 'Be strong, fear not! Behold, your God will come with vengeance, with the divine recompense. He will come and save you.'

Then shall the eyes of the blind be opened, and the ears of the deaf unstopped; then the lame shall leap like a deer, and the tongue of the dumb speak for joy. For waters shall break forth in the wilderness, and streams in the desert; the burning sand shall become a pool, and the thirsty ground springs of water.

Isaiah 35: 1–7a

If you prefer to take a different Bible reading each day, there is a full list of suggested passages at the back of the book (pages 238–254). The readings for Advent are on pages 238–239.

Advent

Pause for reflection

The Benedictus (Song of Zechariah)

1 Blessed be the Lord God of Israel:
   for he has visited and redeemed his people.

2 He has raised up for us a mighty Saviour:
   born of the house of his servant, David.

3 As he spoke through his holy prophets of old:
   that we should be saved from our enemies,
   from the hands of all who hate us;

4 To perform the mercy promised to our fathers:
   and to remember his holy covenant,

5 The oath which he swore to our father Abraham:
   to deliver us from the hand of our enemies;

6 That we might serve him without fear:
   holy and righteous in his sight all the days of our life.

7 And you, my child, will be called the prophet of the
   Most High:
   for you will go before the Lord to prepare his way,

8 To give his people knowledge of salvation:
   through the forgiveness of their sins.

9 In the tender compassion of our God:
   the dawn from on high shall break upon us,

10 To give light to those who sit in darkness and the
   shadow of death:
   and to guide our feet into the way of peace.

Luke 1: 68–79

Glory to the Father, and to the Son:
   and to the Holy Spirit;
as it was in the beginning, is now:
   and shall be for ever. Amen.

OR

The Great Os of Advent

*These prayers originate in the Advent Antiphons, an ancient
part of the Church's liturgy, sung at Evensong from 17 to 23
December as part of the preparation for Christmas. They can be
used separately or as a sequence.*

O WISDOM, mysterious Word of God,
   coming forth from the Father
   and filling all creation with your life-giving power:
Come and show us the way of truth.   *(17 Dec.)*

O LORD OF ISRAEL, ruler of your ancient people,
   you appeared to Moses in the burning bush
   and gave the law on Mount Sinai:
Come, and reach out your hand to save us.   *(18 Dec.)*

O FLOWER OF JESSE'S LINE, Son of David,
   you have been lifted up as a sign of peace,
   drawing all kings and peoples to stand silent in your
      presence:
Come quickly and help us we beseech you.   *(19 Dec.)*

O KEY OF DAVID, and sceptre of the house of Israel,
   you have opened to us the way of hope,
   and shut the door on the powers of evil:
Come and free us from our prisons of darkness.
                                            (20 Dec.)

O MORNING STAR, radiance of the Father's love,
  you are the brightness that disperses the shadows of our
    hearts:
Come, cleanse and renew us in your glory.   *(21 Dec.)*

O KING OF THE NATIONS, you alone bring joy when
    you reign in our hearts,
  and you are the cornerstone of our lives:
Come and strengthen us, who were formed by you.

                                              (22 Dec.)

O EMMANUEL, God with us,
  hope of the world, and Saviour of all,
    come and live in us, now and for ever.   *(23 Dec.)*

PRAYERS

Lord have mercy: in you I trust;
Christ have mercy: on you I depend;
Lord have mercy: you are my peace.

THE LORD'S PRAYER

I give thanks . . .

I confess . . .

I ask for help and guidance . . .

I pray for those I love . . .
        for people I encounter in my daily life . . .
        for those carrying responsibilities . . .
        for those in need or distress . . .

Daily Prayer

God of all hope and joy,
open our hearts in welcome,
that your Son Jesus Christ at his coming
may find in us a dwelling prepared for himself;
who lives and reigns with you and the Holy Spirit,
one God now and for ever.

A New Zealand Prayer Book

O R

Come, O Christ my Light, and illumine my darkness.
Come, my Life, and revive me from death.
Come, my Physician, and heal my wounds.
Come, Flame of divine love, and burn up the thorns of my
    sins,
kindling my heart with the fire of your love.
For you alone are my King and my Lord.

St Dimitrii of Rostov (17th century)

Conclusion

I will bless the Lord: thanks be to God.
Maranatha!* Come, Lord Jesus!

* A prayer in Aramaic, the language spoken by Jesus and his
disciples, meaning 'O Lord, come!' This became a watchword
among the early Christians (1 Corinthians 16: 22).

A QUIET SPACE

Some suggestions for meditation and other ways of praying

Before you start

Spend some time being still and resting in God's presence. As a help, to lead you into quietness:

- sit comfortably with your back fairly straight;
- release the tension in your neck and head, and then in all of your body;
- listen to the sounds around you, first the distant ones, then the nearer ones.

Wait quietly on God;

trust him;

let yourself go into his hands.

You might like to say quietly to yourself the name 'Jesus' or 'Lord' or 'Abba, Father' with the rhythm of your breathing.

Be still, and know that I am God. (Psalm 46: 10)

* * *

You will not necessarily find all the following ideas helpful. Use the ones that are right for you. But having chosen a meditation or passage, it is probably best to stick to it, rather than chopping and changing.

Quiet Space

1. Prayerful reading

Take today's short Scripture passage under *A Thread for the Day,* or all or part of the longer reading in the suggestions for the year on pages 238–254, and follow the way known as *Lectio Divina*, literally 'Divine' or 'Spiritual Reading' – see Appendix B on page 264.

* * *

2. To ponder – The Surprise of the Incarnation

Lord Jesus Christ,
you came to a stable
when men looked in a palace;
you were born in poverty
when we might have anticipated riches.
King of all the earth,
you were content to visit one nation.
From beginning to end
you upturned our human values
and held us in suspense.
Come to us, Lord Jesus.
Do not let us take you for granted
or pretend that we ever fully understand you.
Continue to surprise us
so that, kept alert,
we are always ready
to receive you as Lord and to do your will.

Donald Hilton

* * *

3. Make an Advent wreath to use at home

A circle of greenery (a foretaste of the evergreens of Christmas, a reminder of the life that never dies)

Four white candles (each one representing a thanksgiving – see below)

A central, gold candle (to light on Christmas Day, a sign of Christ, God with us)

The flame is an important symbol of the coming of Christ, the true Light, into our dark world. Light a new candle each week as a sign of expectation, and thanksgiving for:

Week 1: the ways in which the Old Testament prophets anticipated Christ's coming

Week 2: Mary's utter openness and obedience to God

Week 3: John the Baptist's brave witness to Jesus

Week 4: the spreading of the light of Christ through the ancient world and right up to the present day

Each time you light the candle, you could join with family or friends, perhaps before a meal, staying quietly with the candles for a while, and saying a prayer such as:

In silence and awe we await your coming, glorious Lord of heaven and earth. Amen.

* * *

4. Prayer as attention, prayer as waiting

It has been said that the heart of prayer is *attention*, being radically open to God.

Prayer also involves *waiting*, lovingly and trustingly, like parched earth waiting patiently for the rain to fall.

Quiet Space

Lord, I surrender to you all my anxieties and burdens, my hopes and responsibilities.

I give you my full attention; help me simply
  to wait upon you,
  to trust you,
  to rest in you.

In the depths of my being I become quiet and still;
I wait for you, my God, source of my salvation.

Based on Psalm 62: 1

The one who is present everywhere and fills everything is coming. He is coming to fulfil among you the salvation offered to all. Welcome him who welcomed everything that pertains to our human nature.

St Andrew of Crete (c. 660–740)

*   *   *

NIGHT-TIME BLESSING

Be, O Lord, a bright flame before me,
    a guiding star above me,
    a smooth path below me,
    a kindly shepherd behind me,
today – tonight – and for ever. Amen.

St Columba (c. 521–97)

Christmas

CHRISTMAS

Christmas Day to 5 January

We celebrate not only the infant's birth in Bethlehem, but also the unconquerable hope for all time, given to us by the 'becoming flesh' of God's Son.

A THREAD FOR THE DAY

Sunday

The angel said to the shepherds, 'Do not be afraid. Behold, I bring you good news of great joy, which shall be to all people; for to you is born this day, in the city of David, a Saviour, who is Christ the Lord.'

Luke 2: 10–11

Monday

Behold, a virgin shall conceive and bear a son, and shall call his name Immanuel, 'God with us'.

Isaiah 7: 14b

Tuesday

Mary said to the angel, 'Behold, I am the servant of the Lord. Let it be unto me according to your word.'

Luke 1: 38a

Wednesday

Be silent, all people, in the presence of the Lord! For he has stirred himself and is coming from his holy dwelling-place.

Zechariah 2: 13

Thursday

When all things were in quiet stillness, and the night was in the midst of her swift course, your almighty Word leaped down from heaven, out of your royal throne.

Wisdom 18: 14–15a

Friday

'I will make a covenant of peace with them,' says the Lord. 'It shall be an everlasting covenant, and I will bless them and multiply them, and set my sanctuary in the midst of them for ever. My dwelling-place shall be with them; and I will be their God and they shall be my people.'

Ezekiel 37: 26–7

Saturday

In the beginning was the Word, and the Word was with God, and the Word was God. And the Word became flesh, and dwelt among us; and we beheld his glory, as of the Father's only Son, full of grace and truth.

John 1: 1, 14

A SHORT ORDER OF DAILY PRAYER

A moment of quiet: be still and know that God is here.

Begin with today's short piece of Scripture, under
A Thread for the Day, *and reflect on that for a moment.*

Lord, touch my lips:
    that I may sing your praise with all my heart.

You are the light of hope dawning in the world:
    deliver us from darkness and despair.

Glory to God, Father, Son and Holy Spirit:
    mystery of love, behind, through and beyond all things.

For the wonder of your coming I praise you:
    with choirs of angels I worship you.

As I turn my face to you, O God,
let my worship be once more a new beginning:
cleanse my spirit in your mercy,
draw me ever deeper into your love,
and accept my offering of praise and prayer
on behalf of the world;
through Jesus Christ,
our Brother and our Saviour. Amen.

Psalm 46

1 God is our refuge and strength:
   a very present help in trouble.

2 Therefore we will not fear, though the earth be moved:
   and though the mountains shake in the midst of the
      sea;

3 Though its waters rage and foam:
   and though the mountains tremble at its tumult.

4 There is a river whose streams make glad the city of
      God:
   the holy dwelling-place of the Most High.

5 God is in the midst of her, she shall not be overthrown:
   God will help her at daybreak.

6 The nations rage and the kingdoms are shaken:
   God has spoken, and the earth shall melt away.

7 The Lord of hosts is with us:
   the God of Jacob is our refuge.

8 Come and behold what the Lord has done:
   what destruction he has wrought upon the earth.

9 He makes wars to cease in all the world:
   he breaks the bow and shatters the spear,
      and burns the chariots with fire.

10 'Be still, and know that I am God:
   I will be exalted among the nations,
      I will be exalted in the earth.'

11 The Lord of hosts is with us:
the God of Jacob is our refuge.

Unshakeable Creator,
hold us firmly in this unstable world;
help us to be still
and know that you are God,
dwelling in the midst of us
in Jesus Christ, our Lord. Amen.

OR

Psalm 98

1 O sing to the Lord a new song:
for he has done marvellous things.

2 His right hand and his holy arm:
have won for him the victory.

3 The Lord has made known his salvation:
he has revealed his righteousness in the sight of the
nations.

4 He has remembered his steadfast love and faithfulness
to the house of Israel:
and all the ends of the earth
have seen the salvation of our God.

5 Make a joyful noise to the Lord, all the earth:
break into song and make melody.

6 Sing to the Lord with the harp:
with the harp and with songs of praise.

7 With trumpets and the sound of the horn:
   shout with joy before the King, the Lord.

8 Let the sea roar, and all that is in it:
   the earth and those who dwell on it.

9 Let the rivers clap their hands:
   let the mountains ring out with joy before the Lord.

10 For he comes to judge the earth:
   and he shall judge the world with righteousness,
      and the peoples with equity.

   In union with the song of all creation
   I lift my heart in praise to you, O Christ,
   for you have come into the world
   to bring us hope and freedom;
   blessèd are you, our Saviour and Lord. Amen.

Other psalms suitable for **Christmas** are numbers 2, 85, 89 (in two halves), 113, 147.

Or you may want to use a psalm with a particular theme, see pages 235–237.

At the end of the psalm you could use one of the psalm prayers above, or the Gloria:

Glory to the Father, and to the Son:
   and to the Holy Spirit;
as it was in the beginning, is now:
   and shall be for ever. Amen.

SCRIPTURE READING

In the beginning was the Word, and the Word was with God, and the Word was God. He was in the beginning with God. All things were made through him, and without him was not anything made that was made. In him was life, and the life was the light of all. The light shines in the darkness, and the darkness has not overcome it. And the Word became flesh and dwelt among us, and we have seen his glory, as of the only Son of the Father, full of grace and truth.

John 1: 1–5, 14

OR

But you, O Bethlehem of Ephrathah, you who are one of the little clans of Judah, from you shall come forth for me one who is to rule in Israel, whose origin is from of old, from ancient days. He shall stand and feed his flock in the strength of the Lord, in the majesty of the name of the Lord his God. And they shall live secure, for he shall be great to the ends of the earth.

Micah 5: 2, 4

If you prefer to take a different Bible reading each day, there is a full list of suggested passages at the back of the book (pages 238–254). The Christmas readings are on page 239.

Pause for reflection

The Magnificat (Song of Mary)

1 My soul proclaims the greatness of the Lord:
  my spirit rejoices in God my Saviour.

2 For he has looked with favour on his lowly servant:
   from this day all generations will call me blessèd.

3 The Almighty has done great things for me:
   and holy is his name.

4 He has mercy on those who fear him:
   throughout all generations.

5 He has shown strength with his arm:
   he has scattered the proud in their conceit.

6 He has cast down the mighty from their thrones:
   and has lifted up the lowly.

7 He has filled the hungry with good things:
   and the rich he has sent away empty.

8 He has come to the help of his servant, Israel:
   for he has remembered his promise of mercy.

9 The promise he made to our forebears:
   to Abraham and his children for ever.

Luke 1: 46b–55

Glory to the Father, and to the Son:
   and to the Holy Spirit;
as it was in the beginning, is now:
   and shall be for ever. Amen.

OR

A Song of Earth's Offering

What shall we offer you, O Christ,
who for our sakes appeared on earth as man?
Every creature made by you offers you thanks.

The angels offer you a hymn;
the heavens, a star;

the Magi, gifts;
the shepherds, their wonder;
the earth, a cave.

And from our human race we offered you a Virgin
Mother.
God before all ages, have mercy upon us.

From the Festal Menaion *of the Russian Orthodox Church*

PRAYERS

Lord have mercy: in you I trust;
Christ have mercy: on you I depend;
Lord have mercy: you are my peace.

THE LORD'S PRAYER

I give thanks . . .

I confess . . .

I ask for help and guidance . . .

I pray for those I love . . .
>for people I encounter in my daily life . . .
>for those carrying responsibilities . . .
>for those in need or distress . . .

Son of God, Child of Mary,
born in the stable at Bethlehem,
be born again in us this day,
that through us the world may know
the wonder of your love.

A New Zealand Prayer Book

O R

Jesus, Son of God,
now that we have heard the angels sing,
may we not lose our sense of the joy of heaven;
and now that we have been with the shepherds to
   Bethlehem,
make us witnesses
of the wonder of the love we have seen.
Fill us with the quiet joy of Mary,
so that we, too,
may keep all these things
and ponder them in our hearts.

Conclusion

I will bless the Lord: thanks be to God.
Glory be to God on high! And on earth peace! Amen!

A QUIET SPACE

Some suggestions for meditation and other ways
of praying

Before you start

Spend some time being still and resting in God's presence.
As a help, to lead you into quietness:

– sit comfortably with your back fairly straight;
– release the tension in your neck and head, and then in
  all of your body;
– listen to the sounds around you, first the distant ones,
  then the nearer ones.

Wait quietly on God;
>   trust him;
>   let yourself go into his hands.

You might like to say quietly to yourself the name 'Jesus'
or 'Lord' or 'Abba, Father' with the rhythm of your
breathing.

Be still, and know that I am God. (Psalm 46: 10)

* * *

You will not necessarily find all the following ideas helpful. Use
the ones that are right for you. But having chosen a meditation
or passage, it is probably best to stick to it, rather than chopping
and changing.

Christmas

1. Prayerful reading

Take today's short Scripture passage under *A Thread for the Day,* or all or part of the longer reading in the suggestions for the year on page 239, and follow the way known as *Lectio Divina,* literally 'Divine' or 'Spiritual Reading' – see Appendix B on page 264.

* * *

2. To ponder

Because Jesus came as a fully human being, sharing our humanity, it is *in and through our human-ness* that God's saving power works. The Christian faith is not an escape from ordinary human life into some other-worldly cult, but is a healing of our world from the inside.

> Jesus is the 'enfleshment' (which is what 'incarnation' means) of God in the human race . . . [so] our capacity to believe, to hope and to love, has been changed for ever. . . . God became a human being as the outworking of his eternal purpose of love for the whole of the environment, in order to make that entire environment whole again. And he only gave us sacraments – like Baptism and Eucharist – because these would serve as living signs of what this new life is going to be like, a life in which we are continually washed and fed. . . . All of this, of course, impinges on the Sunday-by-Sunday, week-by-week worship of the Christian community wherever it gathers.

Kenneth Stevenson

For the mystery of your coming among us, I praise you, O Lord. You came in such quiet humility, and yet you changed the world.

In Jesus the mutual interpenetration of divine action and human nature is complete.

Anon.

Let the Indwelling One make a heart-space in you.

From a spiritual director's letter to someone seeking God

* * *

3. An icon of the Virgin Mary with the Child Jesus

If you can get hold of one of these icons, spend some time with it. Like all icons, it has been painted with prayer and fasting, and is intended to be a window into the glory of God, drawing you into the divine presence.

See how calm and reflective Mary's face is, and how the gesture of her free hand is saying to us, 'Look at my Son.' She is pointing away from herself to him, and drawing our gaze into the mystery of the divine presence among us.

On most of these icons, Jesus is seen as an affectionate infant, leaning up to Mary's cheek and touching her shoulder with his hand, sometimes even clinging to her veil in a typical baby movement. This is a glimpse of how utterly human Jesus is. (On some icons Jesus is portrayed as a tiny man, blessing us and holding a scroll of the gospels. This may seem strange and unreal at first, but it is worth persevering and staying with this, as it symbolizes his wholeness as a human being alongside his extra-ordinary humility in becoming small and dependent on the care of a woman, for our sakes.)

You will see a subtle use of gold paint. This represents the heavenly glory, and sunlight or candle-light bring out the glowing quality of the gold even more. Jesus is enfolded in gold throughout his garment, to symbolize his divinity. The glory is also reflected on Mary's cuffs, on the edge of her veil, and on the star above her forehead, representing her virginity.

Mary's distant gaze makes her look almost detached from her son, even though she holds him lovingly, and she seems quite vulnerable. The enormity of her calling means that she can only wonder.

All who heard it were amazed at what the shepherds told them. But Mary treasured all these things and pondered them in her heart (Luke 2: 18–19).

* * *

NIGHT-TIME BLESSING

May the humility of the shepherds,
the perseverance of the wise men,
the joy of the angels,
and the peace of the Christ child
be God's gifts to us and to people everywhere
this Christmas time. Amen.

The Promise of His Glory

Epiphany

EPIPHANY

6 January to 2 February

The weeks of Epiphany deepen our understanding of the Incarnation, as we celebrate the 'epiphany' or 'showing' of Jesus' divine glory to the world, and pray for all Christian mission. The coming of the wise men represents the revealing of the light of Christ to the nations. Two other events are also important at this time: Jesus' baptism in the River Jordan, and the miracle of water turned into wine at Cana. In both of these Jesus' divine nature is revealed. The season ends with the Presentation of the child Jesus in the Temple (2 February); this day marks a change of mood, from our joy at Jesus' birth to our awareness of the cost of it all, as we begin to look towards Lent. (There is a special prayer for the Presentation of Jesus in Appendix A.)

A THREAD FOR THE DAY

Sunday

Wise men came from the East to Jerusalem saying, 'Where is he who has been born king of the Jews?'

Matthew 2: 1b–2a

Monday

Jesus said, 'I am the light of the world; whoever follows

me will not walk in darkness, but will have the light of life.'

John 8: 12

Tuesday

When they saw the star they rejoiced greatly, and, going into the house, they saw the child, with Mary his mother, and fell down and worshipped him. And they opened their treasures and offered him gifts, gold, frankincense and myrrh.

Matthew 2: 10–11

Wednesday

We preach not ourselves, but Jesus Christ as Lord. For it is the God who said, 'Let light shine out of darkness,' who has shone in our hearts to give the light of the knowledge of the glory of God in the face of Christ.

2 Corinthians 4: 5a, 6

Thursday

Behold my servant whom I uphold,
    my chosen, in whom my soul delights;
I have put my Spirit upon him,
    and he will bring forth justice to the nations.

Isaiah 42: 1

Friday

The Lord says to me, who formed me from the womb to be his servant, 'It is too light a thing that you should raise up the tribes of Jacob and restore the survivors of Israel; I will give you as a light to the nations that my salvation may reach to the ends of the earth.'

Isaiah 49: 5a, 6

Saturday

Having been warned in a dream not to return to Herod, the wise men returned home another way.

Matthew 2: 12

A SHORT ORDER OF DAILY PRAYER

A moment of quiet: be still and know that God is here.

Begin with today's short piece of Scripture, under
A Thread for the Day, and reflect on that for a moment.

Lord, touch my lips:
    that I may sing your praise with all my heart.

Shine in my soul, O Light of the world:
    come to my aid, O Saviour and Lord.

Glory to God, Father, Son and Holy Spirit:
    mystery of love, behind, through and beyond all things.

I will worship the Lord in the beauty of holiness:
    praise to you, Christ, beloved Son of God.

As I turn my face to you, O God,
let my worship be once more a new beginning:
cleanse my spirit in your mercy,
draw me ever deeper into your love,
and accept my offering of praise and prayer
on behalf of the world;
through Jesus Christ,
our Brother and our Saviour. Amen.

Psalm 67

1 God be merciful unto us and bless us:
   and make the light of your countenance shine upon us;

2 That your ways may be known upon earth:
   your saving health among all nations.

3 Let the peoples praise you, O God:
   let all the peoples praise you.

4 Let the nations be glad and sing for joy:
   for you judge the peoples with equity,
      and govern the nations upon earth.

5 Let the peoples praise you, O God:
   let all the peoples praise you.

6 Then shall the earth bring forth her increase:
   and God, even our own God, shall give us his blessing.

7 God shall bless us:
   and all the ends of the earth shall stand in awe of him.

Bless us, O God, as we labour
for peace and justice
on this your fruitful earth,
that the nations may see your glory
and praise your name for ever,
through Jesus Christ, our Lord. Amen.

OR

Psalm 138

1 I will give thanks to you, O Lord, with my whole heart:
before the gods will I sing your praise.

2 I will bow down towards your holy temple, and give
thanks to your name:
because of your steadfast love and faithfulness.

3 For you have exalted your name:
and your word above all things.

4 All the kings of the earth shall praise you, O Lord:
for they have heard the words of your mouth,

5 And they shall sing of the ways of the Lord:
for great is the glory of the Lord.

6 For though the Lord is high, he cares for the lowly:
as for the proud, he perceives them from afar.

7 Though I walk in the midst of trouble, you will preserve
my life:
you will stretch out your hand against the wrath of my
enemies,
and your right hand will deliver me.

8 The Lord will fulfil his purpose for me:
your steadfast love, O Lord, endures for ever;
do not forsake the work of your hands.

God of the great and the lowly,
guide me on my journey through life:
give me strength to withstand evil and temptation,
and complete your loving purposes for me,
through the saving power of Jesus Christ, my Lord.
Amen.

Other psalms suitable for **Epiphany** are numbers 2, 29, 45, 47, 48, 72, 96, 99.

Or you may want to use a psalm with a particular theme, see pages 235–237.

At the end of the psalm you could use one of the psalm prayers above, or the Gloria:

Glory to the Father, and to the Son:
    and to the Holy Spirit;
as it was in the beginning, is now:
    and shall be for ever. Amen.

SCRIPTURE READING

Arise, shine; for your light has come, and the glory of the Lord has risen upon you. For darkness shall cover the earth, and thick darkness the peoples; but the Lord will arise upon you, and his glory will appear over you.

Nations shall come to your light, and kings to the brightness of your dawn. Lift up your eyes and look around; they all gather together, they come to you; your sons shall come from far away, and your daughters shall be carried on their nurses' arms.

Then you shall see and be radiant; your heart shall thrill and rejoice, because the abundance of the sea shall be brought to you, the wealth of the nations shall come to you. A multitude of camels shall cover your land, the young camels of Midian and Ephah; all those from Sheba shall come. They shall bring gold and frankincense, and shall proclaim the praise of the Lord.

Isaiah 60: 1–6

Epiphany

OR

Then Jesus came from Galilee to John at the Jordan, to be baptised by him. John would have prevented him, saying 'I need to be baptised by you, and do you come to me?' But Jesus answered him, 'Let it be so for now; for it is right for us in this way to fulfil all righteousness.' Then he consented. And when Jesus had been baptised, just as he came up from the water, suddenly the heavens were opened to him and he saw the Spirit of God descending like a dove and alighting on him. And a voice from heaven said, 'This is my Son, the Beloved, with whom I am well pleased.'

Matthew 3: 13–17

If you prefer to take a different Bible reading each day, there is a full list of suggested passages at the back of the book (pages 238–254). The Epiphany readings are on page 240.

Pause for reflection

Nunc Dimittis (Song of Simeon)

1 Now, Lord, you let your servant go in peace:
   your word has been fulfilled.

2 My own eyes have seen the salvation:
   which you have prepared in the sight of every people:

3 A light to reveal you to the nations:
   and the glory of your people Israel.

Luke 2: 29–32

Glory to the Father, and to the Son:
   and to the Holy Spirit;
as it was in the beginning, is now:
   and shall be for ever. Amen.

54

OR

A Song of God's Holiness

Worthy are you, our Lord and our God,
  to receive glory and honour and power.

For you created all things,
  and by your will they exist and have their being.

Worthy are you, O Lamb of God, for you were slain,
  and by your blood you have redeemed
  those of every tribe, language, people and nation.

You made them into a kingdom,
  and into priests serving our God.

And they shall reign with you on earth
  for ever and ever. Amen.

Based on Revelation 4: 11, 5: 9b–10

PRAYERS

Lord have mercy: in you I trust;
Christ have mercy: on you I depend;
Lord have mercy: you are my peace.

THE LORD'S PRAYER

I give thanks . . .

I confess . . .

I ask for help and guidance . . .

Epiphany

I pray for those I love . . .
for people I encounter in my daily life . . .
for those carrying responsibilities . . .
for those in need or distress . . .

All-loving God,
who led the wise men to Bethlehem:
guide us, your people, on our journey of faith,
that we may live according to your will
and witness to the joy of the gospel,
in the name of Jesus Christ our Lord. Amen.

O R

Lord Jesus,
I offer you the gold of my desire to love,
even though I am often uncaring;
I offer you the incense of my longing to pray,
although my spirit can be lukewarm;
I offer you the myrrh of my troubles and frustrations,
even when self-pity and bitterness creep in.
Receive and make good my gifts,
and grant that I may, like the wise men,
find some kneeling-space at Bethlehem.

Conclusion

Let all the world praise and bless the Lord!
Thanks be to God. Amen.

A QUIET SPACE

Some suggestions for meditation and other ways of praying

Before you start

Spend some time being still and resting in God's presence. As a help, to lead you into quietness:

- sit comfortably with your back fairly straight;
- release the tension in your neck and head, and then in all of your body;
- listen to the sounds around you, first the distant ones, then the nearer ones.

Wait quietly on God;
> trust him;
>> let yourself go into his hands.

You might like to say quietly to yourself the name 'Jesus' or 'Lord' or 'Abba, Father' with the rhythm of your breathing.

Be still, and know that I am God. (Psalm 46: 10)

* * *

You will not necessarily find all the following ideas helpful. Use the ones that are right for you. But having chosen a meditation or passage, it is probably best to stick to it, rather than chopping and changing.

Epiphany

1. Prayerful reading

Take today's short Scripture passage under *A Thread for the Day,* or all or part of the longer reading in the suggestions for the year on page 240, and follow the way known as *Lectio Divina,* literally 'Divine' or 'Spiritual Reading' – see Appendix B on page 264.

* * *

2. True wisdom

In a sermon about the setbacks faced by the wise men, Michael Stancliffe considers their disappointments in the Jerusalem palace: they found no young prince; there was no eager welcome for them; nobody offered them any further help, other than the instruction to go to the small and unlikely town of Bethlehem . . .

> With that, they were shown to the door and into the night. However, none of those things led them to despair or to lose their faith – for they were wise men. They were not ashamed to admit the limits of their knowledge or the incompleteness of their faith – for they were wise men. . . . And even though the information perhaps seemed unlikely to be relevant, the travellers were ready to attend to that information and put it to the test – for they were wise men. And so it came to pass that, when the bright lights of Herod's palace were behind them and they were out again in the dark, the original revelation was renewed and 'the star which they saw in the East went before them till it came and stood over where the young child was.' Even so,

Lord, make us wise, confirm our faith, and lead us to thyself.

* * *

3. An ancient hymn

This splendid yet little known hymn dates from the fifth century, and deserves prayerful reflection. It picks up three traditional strands in the season of Epiphany, i.e. the coming of the wise men, the baptism of Jesus in the Jordan, and the miracle at the wedding feast of Cana; each of these events is a 'revealing' or 'epiphany' of the divine glory of Jesus.

You might like to meditate slowly on the words:

Why, impious Herod, shouldst thou fear
Because the Christ is come so near?
He who doth heavenly kingdoms grant
Thine earthly realm can never want.

Lo, sages from the East are gone
To where the star hath newly shone:
Led on by light to Light they press,
And by their gifts their God confess.

The Lamb of God is manifest
Again in Jordan's water blest,
And he who sin had never known
By washing hath our sins undone.

Yet he that ruleth everything
Can change the nature of the spring,
And gives at Cana this for sign –
The water reddens into wine.
Then glory, Lord, to thee we pay

For thine Epiphany to-day;
All glory through eternity
To Father, Son and Spirit be. Amen.

C. Sedulius, written c. 450.

*   *   *

4. Prayer with a candle: 'we have seen his glory'

During Epiphany we celebrate the revealing of the divine glory in the world.

- Light a candle. Ask God to fill you with his radiance.

- Read slowly these words of Evelyn Underhill:

  Prayer is being delicately luminous with the Love of God, in which we live and move and have our being. . . . There is a mighty movement of the Divine generosity running right through the spiritual world, using as its agents the loving and surrendered souls of human beings.

Lord make me transparent with your light; use my prayers to bring your light to others.

*   *   *

5. To ponder

All the paths from East to West, from morning to evening, lead us on through the deserts of life, with all its changes. But these paths can be turned into the blessed pilgrimage – the journey to God. Set out, begin the journey. You can't take much with you, and you will lose much on the way. Let it go. Gold of love, incense of yearning, myrrh of suffering – these you certainly have with you. He will accept them, and you will find him.

Mother Jane Margaret CSMV, d. 1972

*   *   *

6. The Three Kings

If possible, listen to a recording of the song *The Three Kings* (words and music by Peter Cornelius, 1824–74). Many cathedral choirs have recorded it, and also the choir of King's College, Cambridge, who sometimes sing it during their broadcast carol service on Christmas Eve.

Play the music and follow the words as you listen, entering into the praise that is offered. (You could use these words anyway, even without a recording.)

The soloist tells the story:

Three kings from Persian lands afar,
To Jordan follow the pointing star;
And this the quest of the travellers three,
Where the new-born King of the Jews may be;
Full royal gifts they bear for the king:
Gold, incense, myrrh are their offering.

In the background, the choir sings the chorale:

How brightly shines the morning star,
With grace and truth from heaven afar. . . .
Of Jacob's stem and David's line,
For thee, my bridegroom, King divine,
My soul with love o'er-floweth.
Thy word, Jesu,

Inly feeds us, rightly leads us, life bestowing.
Praise, O praise such love o'er-flowing.

The soloist continues the story, and ends with the words:

Offer thy heart to the infant King;
Offer thy heart.

*   *   *

7. An icon of the Baptism of Jesus by John in the Jordan

If you can get hold of one of these icons, spend some time with it. Like all icons, it has been painted with prayer and fasting, and is intended to be a window into the glory of God, drawing you into the divine presence.

The icon shows us that this moment marks the beginning of the manifestation or 'epiphany' of Jesus at the beginning of his public ministry. When Jesus voluntarily descends into the river the voice of the Father acclaims him, 'This is my beloved Son.' So the descent of the dove (the Holy Spirit) is central and prominent, descending from heaven in a powerful ray which emanates from a segment of a circle, representing the divine realm.

The River Jordan is in a deep, dark gorge carved out between steep mountains, and looks rather like a tomb, symbolizing Jesus' willingness to descend into the darkness of our human condition so that his redeeming love can triumph. Thus this moment prefigures his death and the ultimate defeat of Satan and the powers of evil. The paradox is clearly shown that, when Jesus is highly vulnerable and enters the black waters in total obedience (emptying himself, cf. Philippians 2: 7), he emerges with serene majesty as the declared Son of God.

With his right hand Jesus is making a sign of blessing. He blesses the water and sanctifies it; from now on, the waters no longer signify chaos and death (the traditional Hebrew view of the waters of the abyss), but are transformed into something life-giving – the waters of baptism offering us all new life in Christ.

The small, allegorical figures that are sometimes painted in the river represent the Jordan and the Red Sea. Angels look on in wonder and awe, and, in an interesting detail, their hands are covered with their own cloaks, as a sign of reverence at the unfathomable humility of the divine Son.

John the Baptist said, 'He must increase but I must decrease.' (John 3: 30)

Today Christ has come to be baptised in Jordan. The powers of heaven are amazed as they behold the marvellous mystery. And we who have been enlightened receive his light and cry aloud, 'Glory to God made manifest, who has appeared on earth and brought light to the world.'

From the Orthodox Festal Menaion

*   *   *

8. The Presentation of the Child Jesus in the Temple

On or near 2 February, read again the story of Simeon and Anna in the Jerusalem Temple, two faithful contemplatives who had waited in trust and had at last found fulfilment of their hopes (Luke 2: 22–38).

Reflect upon Simeon's joyful abandon and readiness for death, because he has now seen God's Son, the Saviour and light of the world. In your imagination, watch him gently taking the child Jesus from Mary's arms. Look at his face. And watch Mary and Joseph too. Then old Anna comes hobbling forward, equally happy. Stay with that moment. What strikes you most about the whole scene?

You may find it helpful to write down what happened during these exercises, and, at some point, to talk about it with a friend or spiritual director.

*   *   *

NIGHT-TIME BLESSING

Bless to us O God the road that is before us.
Bless to us O God the friends who are around us.
Bless to us O God your love which is within us.
Bless to us O God the light that leads us home.

Ruth Burgess

Ordinary Time 1

ORDINARY TIME 1

3 February to Shrove Tuesday

This period is a chance to draw breath between the celebrations surrounding Jesus' birth and the challenging themes of Lent, Holy Week and Easter. If Ash Wednesday falls early in the year, Ordinary Time I will only last for a few days; at other times it can last for a month or more.

A THREAD FOR THE DAY

Sunday

O the depth of the riches and wisdom and knowledge of God! How unsearchable are his judgements and how inscrutable his ways! To him be glory for ever. Amen.

Romans 11: 33, 36b

Monday

I have been crucified with Christ; it is no longer I who live, but Christ who lives in me.

Galatians 2: 19b–20a

Tuesday

God forbid that I should boast, save in the cross of our Lord Jesus Christ, through whom the world has been crucified to me, and I to the world.

Galatians 6: 14

Ordinary Time 1

Wednesday

Jesus said, 'You did not choose me, but I chose you. And I appointed you to go and bear fruit, fruit that will last.'

John 15: 16a

Thursday

'I have loved you with an everlasting love,' says the Lord. 'Therefore I have continued my faithfulness towards you.'

Jeremiah 31: 3b

Friday

Do you not know that you are God's temple, and that God's Spirit dwells in you?

1 Corinthians 3: 16

Saturday

Surely God is my salvation; I will trust and will not be afraid, for the Lord God is my strength and my might.

Isaiah 12: 2a

A SHORT ORDER OF DAILY PRAYER

A moment of quiet: be still and know that God is here.

*Begin with today's short piece of Scripture, under
A Thread for the Day, and reflect on that for a moment.*

Lord, touch my lips:
    that I may sing your praise with all my heart.

O God make speed to save me:
    O Lord, come to my aid.

Glory to God, Father, Son and Holy Spirit:
    mystery of love, behind, through and beyond all things.

I will worship the Lord:
    all praise to his name.

As I turn my face to you, O God,
let my worship be once more a new beginning:
cleanse my spirit in your mercy,
draw me ever deeper into your love,
and accept my offering of praise and prayer
on behalf of the world;
through Jesus Christ,
our Brother and our Saviour. Amen.

Psalm 36: 5–12

1 Your steadfast love, O Lord, reaches to the heavens:
  and your faithfulness to the clouds.

2 Your righteousness is like the strong mountains:
  and your justice is like the great deep,
    you save animals and humans alike.

3 How precious is your steadfast love, O Lord:
  all people will take refuge under the shadow of your
    wings.

4 They feast on the abundance of your house:
  and you give them drink from the river of your delights.

5 For with you is the well of life:
  and in your light we shall see light.

6 O continue your steadfast love towards those who
    know you:
  and your saving help to those who are true of heart.

7 Do not let the foot of the proud come against me:
  nor the hand of the wicked drive me away.

8 See, they have fallen down, those who do evil:
  they are cast down, and cannot rise.

At all times and in all places I will trust you,
O merciful and steadfast God:
keep me in your care,
help me when I face injustice,
and save me from the lure
of hate and revenge,
through Jesus Christ, my Lord. Amen.

OR

Psalm 139: 1–17, 23–4

1 Lord, you have searched me out and known me:
   you know when I sit down and when I rise up,
      you comprehend my thoughts long before.

2 You know my path and the places where I rest:
   and are acquainted with all my ways.

3 For even before a word is on my tongue:
   you, Lord, know it altogether.

4 You encompass me behind and before:
   and lay your hand upon me.

5 Such knowledge is too wonderful for me:
   so high that I cannot grasp it.

6 Where shall I go from your Spirit:
   or where can I flee from your presence?

7 If I ascend to heaven you are there:
   if I make the grave my bed, you are there also.

8 If I take the wings of the morning:
   and dwell in the uttermost parts of the sea,

9 even there your hand shall lead me:
   your right hand shall hold me.

10 If I say, 'The darkness will surely cover me:
   and the night will enfold me,'

11 the darkness is not dark to you:
   the night is as bright as day,
      the darkness and light are both alike to you.

12 For you created my inward parts:
   you knit me together in my mother's womb.

13 I will praise you, for I am marvellously made:
   I was formed in secret, intricately woven in the depths
      of the earth.

14 Your eyes saw my limbs when they were still
      incomplete:
   every one of them was written in your book.

15 How deep are your thoughts to me, O God:
   how great is the sum of them!

16 Search me, O God, and know my heart:
   try me and know my thoughts.

17 See if there is any wickedness in me:
   and lead me in the way that is everlasting.

All-seeing and ever-present God,
I thank you
for the wonder of my existence;
you knew me before I was born
and will welcome me when I die,
keep me always in the love of your Son,
Jesus Christ, my Lord. Amen.

*During **Ordinary Time 1** you may also want to use a psalm with
a particular theme, see pages 235–237.*

Daily Prayer

At the end of the psalm you could use one of the psalm prayers above, or the Gloria:

Glory to the Father, and to the Son:
 and to the Holy Spirit;
as it was in the beginning, is now:
 and shall be for ever. Amen.

SCRIPTURE READING

In the beginning God created the heavens and the earth. The earth was without form and void, and darkness covered the face of the deep; and the Spirit of God was moving over the face of the waters. And God said, 'Let there be light'; and there was light. And God saw that the light was good; and God separated the light from the darkness. God called the light Day, and the darkness he called Night. And there was evening and there was morning, the first day.

And God said, 'Let there be a firmament in the midst of the waters, and let it separate the waters from the waters.' So God made the firmament and separated the waters that were beneath it from the waters that were above it. And it was so. God called the firmament Sky. And there was evening and there was morning, a second day.

Genesis 1: 1–8

OR

Now faith is the assurance of things hoped for, the conviction of things not seen. Indeed, by faith our ancestors received approval. By faith we understand that the worlds were prepared by the word of God, so that what is seen was made from things that are not visible.

75

By faith Abraham obeyed when he was called to set out for a place that he was to receive as an inheritance; and he set out, not knowing where he was going. By faith he stayed for a time in a foreign land, living in tents, as did Isaac and Jacob, who were heirs with him of the same promise. For he looked forward to the city that has foundations, whose architect and builder is God.

Hebrews 11: 1–3, 8–10

If you prefer to take a different Bible reading each day, there is a full list of suggested passages at the back of the book (pages 238–254). The readings for Ordinary Time 1 are on pages 241–242.

Pause for reflection

A Song of the Anointing of the Spirit

1 The Spirit of the Lord God is upon me:
 because the Lord has anointed me.

2 He has sent me to bring good news to the poor:
 and to bind up the broken-hearted.

3 To proclaim liberty to the captives:
 and the recovery of sight to the blind.

4 To proclaim the year of the Lord's favour:
 a day of recompense from our God.

5 To comfort all who mourn:
 to give them the oil of gladness instead of mourning.

6 They shall be called oaks of righteousness:
  planted by God for his glory.

7 They shall rebuild the ancient ruins:
  and restore what has long laid waste.

8 For as the earth brings forth shoots and makes new
    things grow:
  the Lord will make integrity and praise spring up before
  all nations.

From Isaiah 61: 1–4,11

Glory to the Father, and to the Son:
  and to the Holy Spirit;
as it was in the beginning, is now:
  and shall be for ever. Amen.

OR

The Jubilate (A Song of Joy)

1 Be joyful in the Lord, all you lands:
  serve the Lord with gladness
    and come before his presence with a song.

2 Know this: the Lord himself is God:
  he himself has made us and we are his;
    we are his people and the sheep of his pasture.

3 Enter his gates with thanksgiving, go into his courts
    with praise:
  give thanks to him and call upon his name.

4 For the Lord is good; his mercy is everlasting:
   and his faithfulness endures from age to age.

Psalm 100

Glory to the Father, and to the Son:
   and to the Holy Spirit;
as it was in the beginning, is now:
   and shall be for ever. Amen.

PRAYERS

Lord have mercy: in you I trust;
Christ have mercy: on you I depend;
Lord have mercy: you are my peace.

THE LORD'S PRAYER

I give thanks . . .

I confess . . .

I ask for help and guidance . . .

I pray for those I love . . .
      for people I encounter in my daily life . . .
      for those carrying responsibilities . . .
      for those in need or distress . . .

O Lord, to be turned from you is to fall, to turn to you
is to rise, and to stand in your presence is to live for
ever. Grant us in all our duties your help, in all our per-

plexities your guidance, in all our dangers your protection, and in all our sorrows your peace; through Jesus Christ our Lord.

St Augustine of Hippo (354–430)

O R

O God of truth and mercy,
whose voice we miss
amidst the distractions and noise of our lives,
penetrate to the core of our being,
that we may hear and be glad,
knowing ourselves accepted in your love,
and able once again to live
in your truth and obedience,
through Jesus Christ our Saviour. Amen.

Jim Cotter

Conclusion

I will bless the Lord:
Thanks be to God.

A QUIET SPACE

Some suggestions for meditation and other ways of praying

Before you start

Spend some time being still and resting in God's presence. As a help, to lead you into quietness:

- sit comfortably with your back fairly straight;
- release the tension in your neck and head, and then in all of your body;
- listen to the sounds around you, first the distant ones, then the nearer ones.

Wait quietly on God;
trust him;
let yourself go into his hands.

You might like to say quietly to yourself the name 'Jesus' or 'Lord' or 'Abba, Father' with the rhythm of your breathing.

Be still, and know that I am God. (Psalm 46: 10)

* * *

You will not necessarily find all the following ideas helpful. Use the ones that are right for you. But having chosen a meditation or passage, it is probably best to stick to it, rather than chopping and changing.

Quiet Space

1. Prayerful reading

Take today's short Scripture passage under *A Thread for the Day*, or all or part of the longer reading in the suggestions for the year on pages 241 to 242, and follow the way known as *Lectio Divina*, literally 'Divine' or 'Spiritual Reading' – see Appendix B on page 264.

* * *

2. To ponder

We do not have to hunt for God; he is the One who is constantly seeking us, and who longs to give himself to us.

You did not choose me; I chose you. (John 15: 16)

> You want to seek God with all your life, and love him with all your heart.
>
> But you would be wrong if you thought you could reach him. Your arms are too short, your eyes are too dim, your heart and understanding too small.
>
> To seek God means first of all to let yourself be found by him.
>
> To choose God is to realize that you are known and loved in a way surpassing anything people can imagine, loved before anyone had thought of you or spoken your name.
>
> To choose God means giving yourself up to him in faith.

Let your life be built on this faith
as on an invisible foundation.

Let yourself be carried by this faith
like a child in its mother's womb.

And so, don't talk too much about God but live in the
certainty that he has written your name on the palm of
his hand.

Rule for a New Brother

* * *

3. An imaginative exercise

In your imagination, be Zacchaeus the tax collector,
climbing a tree in the hope of catching a glimpse of Jesus
of Nazareth as he passes through Jericho (Luke 19: 1–10).

- What do you feel when Jesus stops, looks up at you, and
  invites himself to a meal at your house?
- What happens when Jesus enters *your* home and *your*
  life?

Or place yourself at the front of the crowd at the feeding
of the five thousand (Mark 6: 35–44).

- Offer Jesus your small contribution of food.
- Look at his face when he receives it from you and
  thanks you.
- What happens next?

You may find it helpful to write down what happened during these exercises, and, at some point, to talk about it
with a friend or spiritual director.

* * *

4. To ponder

St Paul depended on the prayers of other Christians, as we, too, depend on the prayers of each other. If I am under stress or my prayer feels weak and inadequate, I can lean on the prayers of others. Similarly, at those times when I am able to spend longer with God, I can trust that my prayer will be used to support and strengthen other members of Christ's body.

As human beings, we affect each other all the time, often in ways we hardly realize; we depend on each other and we belong to each other. So our prayers of intercession are vital within this interconnectedness of all people, and can be a source of blessing to many, often in ways we could not have imagined. Whenever we turn our hearts to God, we bring into our prayer the wounds and struggles of the world to which we belong. Let us ask that we may be caught up in God's healing of all creation.

*Show me, O Lord, how I may play my part
in your body on earth;
use my prayer for my fellow Christians
and for the world.
Thank you for the faithfulness of others
on whom I, in my turn, depend.*

Pray now for any who come to mind.

*   *   *

NIGHT-TIME BLESSING

Into your hands I commend my spirit,
gentle and merciful God;
guard my sleeping, bless my waking,
and be with those I love,
now and always. Amen.

Lent

LENT

Ash Wednesday to the Eve of Palm Sunday

Lent is the time of preparation for Easter, when we focus on penitence, reflection and spiritual growth. From the fourth century this season was of special importance to those awaiting baptism at Easter, and also for people who had been excluded from communion because of some serious sin, and who would be restored on Maundy Thursday. Around the tenth century Lent came to be linked with Christ's forty days of fasting in the wilderness. So it is a time when a renewal of commitment and simple, austere worship are appropriate.

A THREAD FOR THE DAY

Sunday

Thus says the Lord of his people Israel, 'I will allure her and bring her into the wilderness, and speak tenderly to her. There she shall respond as in the days of her youth, as at the time when she came out of the land of Egypt.'

Hosea 2: 14, 15b

Monday

'Fear not, for I have redeemed you; I have called you by name, you are mine. When you pass through the waters I will be with you; and when you walk through fire, the flame shall not consume you. For you are precious in my eyes, and honoured, and I love you,' says the Lord.

From Isaiah 43: 1–4

Tuesday

How long, O Lord? Will you forget me for ever? How long will you hide your face from me? How long must I bear pain in my heart, while my enemy exults over me? But I have trusted in your steadfast love; my heart shall rejoice in your salvation.

Psalm 13: 1–2a, 2c, 5

Wednesday

Thus says the Lord, 'Do not remember the former things, or consider the things of old. I am about to do a new thing; now it springs forth, do you not perceive it? I will make a way in the wilderness, and rivers in the desert, to give drink to my chosen people, the people whom I formed for myself.

Isaiah 43: 18–19, 20b–21a

Thursday

I (Daniel) turned to the Lord God, to seek an answer by prayer and supplication with fasting, sackcloth and ashes. I confessed to him, saying, 'Ah Lord, great and awesome God, keeping covenant and steadfast love with those who love you and keep your commandments, we have sinned and done wrong, rebelling against you. Now therefore, our God, listen to the prayer of your servant, and let your face shine upon your desolated sanctuary, not because of our righteousness but because of your great mercies.

O Lord, hear! O Lord, forgive! Listen and act, and do not delay!'

From Daniel 9: 3–5, 17–19

Friday

If anyone is in Christ, there is a new creation: the old has passed away, and, see, the new has come. All this is from God, who, through Christ, reconciled us to himself. For God was in Christ, reconciling the world to himself, not counting their sins against them, and he has entrusted this message of reconciliation to us.

2 Corinthians 5: 17–19

Saturday

But God, who is rich in mercy, out of the great love with which he loved us, even when we were dead through our sins, has made us alive together with Christ. For by grace you have been saved, through faith; this is not your own doing, it is the gift of God.

Ephesians 2: 4–5a, 8

A SHORT ORDER OF DAILY PRAYER

A moment of quiet: be still and know that God is here.

*Begin with today's short piece of Scripture, under **A Thread for the Day**, and reflect on that for a moment.*

Lord, touch my lips:
    that I may sing your praise with all my heart.

Lord Jesus Christ, have mercy on me:
    deliver me from evil, O Saviour and Redeemer.

Glory to God, Father, Son and Holy Spirit:
    mystery of love, behind, through and beyond all things.

Lord of the wilderness, I worship you:
    all praise to your name. Amen.

As I turn my face to you, O God,
let my worship be once more a new beginning:
cleanse my spirit in your mercy,
draw me ever deeper into your love,
and accept my offering of praise and prayer
on behalf of the world;
through Jesus Christ,
our Brother and our Saviour. Amen.

Psalm 51: 1–11

1 Have mercy on me, O God, in your loving-kindness:
   according to your great mercy, blot out my offences.

2 Wash me thoroughly from my wickedness:
   and cleanse me from my sin.

3 For I acknowledge my transgressions:
   and my sin is ever before me.

4 Against you only have I sinned
      and done what is evil in your sight:
   so that you are justified in your sentence
      and upright in your judgement.

5 Behold I was born in wickedness:
   a sinner when my mother conceived me.

6 You desire truth in the inner being:
   O teach me wisdom in the secret places of my heart.

7 Purge me with hyssop and I shall be clean:
   wash me and I shall be whiter than snow.

8 Let me hear of joy and gladness:
   that the bones which you have broken may rejoice.

9 Hide your face from my sins:
   and blot out all my iniquities.

10 Create in me a clean heart, O God:
   and renew a right spirit within me.

11 Cast me not away from your presence:
   and take not your holy Spirit from me.

Righteous God,
pour your healing and forgiveness
into the core of my being;
purify my heart
and keep me close to you,
through the power of the passion of Jesus Christ,
your Son, our Saviour. Amen.

O R

Psalm 103: 1–18

1 Bless the Lord, O my soul:
   let all that is within me, bless his holy name.

2 Bless the Lord, O my soul:
   and forget not all his benefits.

3 For he forgives all your sins:
   and heals all your diseases.

4 He redeems your life from the Pit:
   and crowns you with mercy and loving-kindness.

5 He satisfies your mouth with good things:
   so that your strength is renewed like an eagle's.

6 The Lord executes righteousness:
   and justice for all who are oppressed.

7 He showed his ways unto Moses:
   his works unto the children of Israel.

8 The Lord is full of compassion and mercy:
   slow to anger and of great goodness.

9 He will not always be chiding us:
   nor will his anger continue for ever.

10 He has not dealt with us according to our sins:
   nor punished us according to our wickedness.

11 For as the heavens are high above the earth:
   so great is his mercy upon those who fear him.

12 As far as the east is from the west:
   so far has he removed our sins from us.

13 As a father has compassion on his children:
   so is the Lord tender towards those who fear him.

14 For he knows what we are made of:
   he remembers that we are but dust.

15 Our mortal days are like the grass:
   we flourish like a flower in the field;

16 when the wind passes over it, it is gone:
   and its place will know it no more.

17 But the steadfast love of the Lord endures for ever on
      those who fear him:
   and his righteousness on their children's children;

18 upon those who keep his covenant:
   and remember and obey his commandments.

Lent

God of infinite gentleness,
have mercy on us your children:
heal all that is broken in us,
and renew our strength
by your unquenchable love,
revealed to us in Jesus Christ
your Son, our Lord. Amen.

Other psalms suitable for **Lent** are numbers 6, 13, 26, 32, 38, 40, 57, 85, 86, 143.

Or you may want to use a psalm with a particular theme, see pages 235–237.

At the end of the psalm you could use one of the psalm prayers above, or the Gloria:

Glory to the Father, and to the Son:
    and to the Holy Spirit;
as it was in the beginning, is now:
    and shall be for ever. Amen.

SCRIPTURE READING

Is not this the fast that I choose: to loose the bonds of wickedness, to undo the thongs of the yoke, to let the oppressed go free, and to break every yoke?

Is it not to share your bread with the hungry, and bring the homeless poor into your house; when you see the naked, to cover them, and not to hide yourself from your own flesh?

Then your light shall break forth like the dawn, and your healing shall spring up quickly; your righteousness shall go before you, the glory of the Lord shall be your rear guard.

Then you shall call, and the Lord will answer; you shall cry, and he will say, 'Here I am.'

Isaiah 58: 6–9

OR

Jesus said, 'No one after lighting a lamp puts it in a cellar or under a bushel, but on a stand, that those who enter may see the light. Your eye is the lamp of your body; when your eye is sound, your whole body is full of light; but when it is not sound, your body is full of darkness. Therefore be careful lest the light in you be darkness. If then your whole body is full of light, it will be wholly bright, as when a lamp with its rays gives you light.'

While he was speaking, a Pharisee asked him to dine with him; so he went in and sat at table. The Pharisee was astonished to see that he did not first wash before dinner. And the Lord said to him, 'Now you Pharisees clean the outside of the cup and of the dish, but inside you are full of greed and wickedness. You fools! Did not the one who made the outside make the inside also? But give for alms those things that are within; and see, everything will be clean for you. But woe to you Pharisees! For you tithe mint and rue and every herb, and neglect justice and the love of God; it is these you ought to have practised without neglecting the others.'

Luke 11: 33–42

If you prefer to take a different Bible reading each day, there is a full list of suggested passages at the back of the book (pages 238–254). The readings for Lent are on pages 242–244.

Pause for reflection

Saviour of the World

1 Jesus, Saviour of the world, come to us in your mercy:
   save us and help us, we humbly beseech you.

2 By your cross and your life laid down, you set your
   people free:
   save us and help us, we humbly beseech you.

3 When they were ready to perish, you saved your
   disciples:
   save us and help us, we humbly beseech you.

4 In the greatness of your mercy loose us from our chains:
   save us and help us, we humbly beseech you.

5 Make yourself known as our Saviour and mighty
   deliverer:
   save us and help us, we humbly beseech you.

6 Come now and dwell with us, Lord Christ Jesus:
   save us and help us, we humbly beseech you.

7 And when you come in your glory, make us one with
   you:
   that we may share the life of your kingdom.

OR

A Litany of Sorrow

Our insensitivity to the needs of others,
                    O Lord, forgive.

Our prejudice and fear, that prevent us from loving,
                    O Lord, forgive.

The narrowness of our vision and our shrinking from your
   demands,
                    O Lord, forgive.

Our resentment against those who have hurt us,
                    O Lord, forgive.

Our desire to do your work in our way,
                    O Lord, forgive.

Our impatience with those who are different from us,
                    O Lord, forgive.

Our failure to listen properly to other points of view,
                    O Lord, forgive.

Our fear of coming out of the fortress of our own souls
   into fuller life and deeper love,
                    O Lord, forgive.

PRAYERS

Lord have mercy: in you I trust;
Christ have mercy: on you I depend;
Lord have mercy: you are my peace.

THE LORD'S PRAYER

I give thanks . . .

I confess . . .

I ask for help and guidance . . .

Lent

I pray for those I love . . .
> for people I encounter in my daily life . . .
> for those carrying responsibilities . . .
> for those in need or distress . . .

Almighty and everlasting God, you despise nothing that you have made and forgive the sins of all who are penitent. Create and make in us new and contrite hearts, that we, worthily lamenting our sins and acknowledging our brokenness, may obtain of you, the God of all mercy, perfect remission and forgiveness; through Jesus Christ our Lord.

Scottish Liturgy

OR

Lord, in these days of mercy, make me quiet and
> prayerful;
in these days of challenge, make me stronger in you;
in these days of emptiness, take possession of me;
in these days of waiting, open my heart to the mystery of
> your cross.

Conclusion

I will bless the Lord, our merciful Creator:
Thanks be to God. Amen.

A QUIET SPACE

Some suggestions for meditation and other ways
of praying

Before you start

Spend some time being still and resting in God's presence.
As a help, to lead you into quietness:

- sit comfortably with your back fairly straight;
- release the tension in your neck and head, and then in
  all of your body;
- listen to the sounds around you, first the distant ones,
  then the nearer ones.

Wait quietly on God;
                    trust him;
                            let yourself go into his hands.

You might like to say quietly to yourself the name 'Jesus'
or 'Lord' or 'Abba, Father' with the rhythm of your
breathing.

Be still, and know that I am God. (Psalm 46: 10)

* * *

You will not necessarily find all the following ideas helpful. Use
the ones that are right for you. But having chosen a meditation
or passage, it is probably best to stick to it, rather than chopping
and changing.

Lent

1. Prayerful reading

Take today's short Scripture passage under *A Thread for the Day*, or all or part of the longer reading in the suggestions for the year on pages 242 to 244, and follow the way known as *Lectio Divina*, literally 'Divine' or 'Spiritual Reading' – see Appendix B on page 264.

* * *

2. Pruning

I am the true vine, and my Father is the vinedresser. Every branch of mine that bears no fruit he takes away, and every branch that does bear fruit he prunes, that it may bear more fruit. I am the vine, you are the branches. Those who abide in me and I in them bear much fruit, because apart from me you can do nothing. (John 15: 1–2, 5)

These words of Jesus invite us to allow God to prune us, out of love, so that we may be more fruitful and creative for him.

I ask God to show me in what ways he wants to prune me.

Do I need to let go of:
old grudges?
habitual negative thoughts about someone or something?
something in my lifestyle that damages me?
too much concern about time, or work?
over-dependence on the good opinion of others?
or . . . ?

Lord, show me what I am grasping too tightly, and give me the grace to let go. All my hope is in you. You are my strength, my delight, my rest and my peace.

These words of Maria Boulding may help in the discernment process:

> Prayer springs from God's life in us. The living God who gives that life himself undertakes the pruning needed for its increase; he prunes through the experience of prayer and the diminishments we suffer in our lives. But he is at work on an intelligent creature whose co-operation is expected. Judicious pruning on your part may therefore also be required, the kind of 'No' to self that will give freer play to life and love. If you give yourself seriously to prayer you will know automatically when something is blocking you and holding you back from God. No elaborate examination of conscience is needed, for it leaps to the eye. It is not your frailties and failures that block, nor your limitations, but anything you hold on to when you know God wants you to let go of it. This is an obvious area for asceticism, though it may also be an area where healing is needed first before you can be free enough to let go.

*   *   *

3. Receiving forgiveness

You might like to work through the following prayer slowly and thoughtfully, in an offering of self-examination and confession.

Lent

Purge me with hyssop and I shall be clean,
Wash me, and I shall be whiter than snow.

(Psalm 51: 7)

Merciful God,
for the things I have done that I regret,
forgive me;
for the things that I have failed to do that I regret,
forgive me;
for all the times I have acted without love,
forgive me;
for all the times I have reacted without thought,
forgive me;
for all the times I have withdrawn care,
forgive me;
for all the times I have failed to forgive,
forgive me.

For hurtful words said and helpful words unsaid,
for unfinished tasks
and unfulfilled hopes,
God of all time
forgive me
and help me
to lay down my burden of regret.

The Pattern of our Days

Now turn your attention away from yourself and on to God, whose loving mercy is pouring out to meet you. Julian of Norwich, fourteenth-century hermit and woman of prayer, spoke of what she saw in her *Revelations of the Divine Love*:

Our gracious Lord does not wish his servants to despair because of frequent or grievous falling, because our falling does not prevent him from loving us.

He is the ground of all our whole life in love, and, furthermore, he is our everlasting protector, and mightily defends us against all our enemies who are most terrible and fierce against us.

He touches us most secretly, and shows us our sin by the sweet light of mercy and grace . . . and then, by the Holy Spirit, we are guided by contrition of prayer and the desire to amend our life. . . . And then our gracious Lord shows himself to the soul, all merrily and with a glad countenance, with friendly greeting, as if the soul had been in pain and prison, saying sweetly thus,

'My dearly beloved, I am glad thou hast come to me. In all thy woe, I have always been with thee, and now thou seest my loving and we are one-ed in bliss.'

* * *

4. The Annunciation of the Angel Gabriel to Mary

Read the account of Mary's response to the Angel Gabriel in Luke 1: 26–38. You could do this on or around 25 March which is the day when we celebrate the 'Annunciation' or 'announcement' from the Angel Gabriel that Mary would bear God's child.

Reflect upon how much depended on Mary's 'Yes'. . .

and how much it cost her.

Ponder the creative tension between being active and being passive, seen supremely in Mary at this moment:

Ask for God's grace to make Mary's words your own.

Behold the servant of the Lord; let it be to me according to your word.

Like sunlight in a burning glass, God's love for us all narrows to a needle of fire, and pierces Mary at Gabriel's salutation.

Austin Farrar (1906–68)

The eternal birth must take place in you.

Meister Eckhart (1260–1327)

* * *

5. To ponder

I can only face up to the fact of the horror of human suffering because of the presence of the Holy One in the middle of all our evil and pain. The agony of our own country is, for me, only bearable because Christ, the Innocent One, was crucified, hung up to die, while his love remained unbroken and undefeated. This enables me to go on loving, and hoping, and planting new crops. In Christ's name and in his power I pray that we shall all find the strength to let love and not hate win the day.

From a sermon by an Anglican priest in Mozambique during the waves of violence and burning of villages in the 1980s.

* * *

6. Cheap grace

Dietrich Bonhoeffer (1905–45) was a German Lutheran pastor and a leading figure in the Confessing Church, the minority Christian movement that resisted the Nazis. In the end he could see no alternative but to become involved in a plot to assassinate Hitler. He and his confederates were caught, and he was hanged on 9 April 1945. During his imprisonment he dug deep into his inner resources, and his remarkable *Letters and Papers from Prison* have been a source of inspiration to many. The following passage is taken from his book *The Cost of Discipleship*:

> Cheap grace is the deadly enemy of our Church. We are fighting today for costly grace. Cheap grace means grace sold on the market like a cheapjack's wares. The sacraments, the forgiveness of sin and the consolations of religion are thrown away at cut prices. Cheap grace is the preaching of forgiveness without requiring repentance, baptism without church discipline, communion without confession, absolution without personal confession. Cheap grace is grace without discipleship, grace without the cross, grace without Jesus Christ, living and incarnate.
>
> Costly grace is the treasure hidden in the field; for the sake of it a man will gladly go and sell all that he has. It is the pearl of great price, to buy which the merchant will sell all his goods. It is the kingly rule of Christ, for whose sake a man will pluck out the eye which causes him to stumble. It is the call of Jesus Christ at which the disciple leaves his nets and follows him.
>
> Such grace is *costly* because it calls us to follow, and it is *grace* because it calls us to follow *Jesus Christ*. It is costly because it costs a man his life, and it is grace because it gives a man the only true life.

* * *

NIGHT-TIME BLESSING

Visit, O Lord, we pray, this place,
and drive far from it all the snares of the enemy.
Let your holy angels dwell here to keep us in peace,
and may your blessing be upon us evermore;
through Jesus Christ our Lord.

The Office of Compline

Holy Week

HOLY WEEK

Palm Sunday to Easter Eve

A THREAD FOR THE DAY

Sunday

Rejoice greatly, O daughter of Zion! Behold, your king is coming to you, humble and riding on an ass.

From Zechariah 9: 9

Monday

St Paul writes, 'We are afflicted in every way, but not crushed; we are perplexed but never in despair; we have been persecuted, but never deserted; knocked down, but not destroyed; always carrying in our body the death of Jesus, so that the life of Jesus, too, may be seen in our body.'

2 Corinthians 4: 8–10

Tuesday

Thus says the Lord, 'O my people, what have I done to you? How have I offended you? Answer me! I led you out of Egypt and redeemed you from slavery, that you might know the power of my saving acts.'

From Micah 6: 3–5

Wednesday

Behold, my servant will prosper, he shall be lifted up and exalted to great heights. Yet the crowds were appalled on seeing him – so disfigured did he look, beyond human semblance. Many were startled at his appearance, and kings stood speechless before him. For he had no form or comeliness that we could see.

From Isaiah 52: 13–15a

Thursday

He was despised and rejected, a man of sorrows and acquainted with grief. Surely ours were the sufferings he bore, ours the sorrows he carried. He was wounded for our sins, and with his stripes we are healed.

From Isaiah 53: 3–5

Friday

When the soldiers found that Jesus was already dead, they did not break his legs; but one of them pierced his side with a spear, and at once there came out blood and water. He who saw it has borne witness, and his testimony is true, that you may believe.

From John 19: 33–5

Saturday

And Joseph of Arimathea, a secret disciple of Jesus, asked Pilate leave to take away the body of Jesus. So he and Nicodemus bound Jesus' body with linen and spices and laid it in a new tomb in the garden.

From John 19: 38–42

A SHORT ORDER OF DAILY PRAYER

A moment of quiet: be still and know that God is here.

Begin with today's short piece of Scripture, under
A Thread for the Day, *and reflect on that for a moment.*

Lord, touch my lips:
  that I may sing your praise with all my heart.

Blessèd are you, O Christ, mocked and broken for us:
  through your cross you give us healing and hope.

Glory to God, Father, Son and Holy Spirit:
  mystery of love, behind, through and beyond all things.

I will worship the Lord:
  all praise to his name.

As I turn my face to you, O God,
let my worship be once more a new beginning:
cleanse my spirit in your mercy,
draw me ever deeper into your love,
and accept my offering of praise and prayer
on behalf of the world;
through Jesus Christ,
our Brother and our Saviour. Amen.

Psalm 22: 1–21

1 My God, my God, why have you forsaken me:
  why are you so far from helping me
    and from the words of my groaning?

2 My God, I cry by day, but you do not answer:
  and by night, but I find no rest.

3 Yet you are eternally holy:
  enthroned on the praises of Israel.

4 Our forebears trusted in you:
  they trusted, and you delivered them.

5 They cried to you, and they were saved:
  they trusted in you, and were not put to shame.

6 But as for me, I am a worm, and hardly human:
  scorned by all, and despised by the people.

7 All those who see me laugh me to scorn:
  they curl their lips at me and shake their heads, saying,

8 'He trusted in the Lord; let him deliver him:
  if he delights in him, let him rescue him.'

9 Yet you are the one who took me out of the womb:
  you kept me safe on my mother's breast.

10 I have been entrusted to you since my birth:
  you were my God when I was in my mother's womb.

11 Be not far from me, for trouble is near:
  and there is no one to help me.

Daily Prayer

12 Many bulls encircle me:
   strong bulls of Bashan surround me.

13 They open wide their mouths at me:
   like a ravening and roaring lion.

14 I am poured out like water
     and all my bones are out of joint:
   my heart is like melting wax within my breast.

15 My mouth is dried up like a potsherd
     and my tongue sticks to the roof of my mouth:
   you lay me in the dust of death.

16 Yea, dogs are all around me,
     a company of evildoers encircles me:
   my hands and my feet are withered.

17 I can count all my bones:
   they stare and gloat at me.

18 They divide my garments among them:
   and cast lots for my clothing.

19 O Lord, do not be far away:
   you are my helper, come quickly to my aid.

20 Deliver my soul from the sword:
   my life from the power of the dog.

21 Save me from the lion's mouth:
   and my soul from the horns of the wild oxen.

God of compassion,
have mercy on all who cry to you
in darkness and despair,
and strengthen us
as we face the cost of discipleship,
in union with your Son,
our Redeemer, Jesus Christ. Amen.

OR

Verses from Psalm 55

1 Hear my prayer, O God:
   do not hide yourself from my petition.

2 Give me your attention and answer me:
   for I am troubled in my complaint.

3 I am distraught by the noise of the enemy:
   because of the onslaught of the wicked.

4 For they bring down disaster upon me:
   and they persecute me with fury.

5 My heart quakes within me:
   the terrors of death have fallen upon me.

6 Fear and trembling come upon me:
   and horror overwhelms me.

7 And I said, 'O for the wings of a dove:
   that I might fly away and be at rest.

8 I would flee far away:
   and I would lodge in the wilderness.

9 I would hasten to find for myself a shelter:
from the stormy wind and tempest.'

10 It is not an enemy who taunted me,
or I might have borne it:
it is not my foe who dealt insolently with me,
for I could have hidden from him.

11 But it was you, one after my own heart:
my companion, my own familiar friend.

12 One with whom I kept pleasant company:
as we walked in the house of our God.

13 But I will call upon God:
and the Lord will save me.

14 At evening and morning, and at noon,
I will utter my complaint and he will hear me.

15 Cast your burden on the Lord, and he will sustain you:
he will never allow the righteous to stumble.

I will trust you, O my God,
and cast my burden upon you
when I am in trouble and alone;
help me to forgive those who hurt me
in the spirit of Jesus your Son,
for your love and your mercy's sake. Amen.

Other psalms suitable for **Holy Week** are numbers 69 (in two halves), 88, 102.

Or you may want to use a psalm with a particular theme, see pages 235–237.

*At the end of the psalm you could use one of the psalm prayers
above, or the Gloria:*

Glory to the Father, and to the Son:
 and to the Holy Spirit;
as it was in the beginning, is now:
 and shall be for ever. Amen.

SCRIPTURE READING

Now before the festival of the Passover, Jesus knew that
his hour had come to depart from this world and go to the
Father. Having loved his own who were in the world, he
loved them to the end. The devil had already put it into the
heart of Judas, son of Simon Iscariot, to betray him. And
during supper, Jesus, knowing that the Father had given all
things into his hands, and that he had come from God and
was going to God, got up from the table, took off his outer
robe, and tied a towel around himself. Then he poured
water into a basin and began to wash the disciples' feet
and to wipe them with the towel that was tied round him.
He came to Simon Peter, who said to him, 'Lord, are you
going to wash my feet?' Jesus answered, 'You do not know
now what I am doing, but later you will understand.' Peter
said to him, 'You will never wash my feet.' Jesus answered,
'Unless I wash you, you have no share in me.' Simon Peter
said to him, 'Lord, not my feet only but also my hands and
my head!' Jesus said to him, 'One who has bathed does not
need to wash, except for the feet, but is entirely clean. And
you are clean, though not all of you.' For he knew who
was to betray him; for this reason he said, 'Not all of you
are clean.'

John 13: 1–11

OR

When he had gone out, Jesus said, 'Now the Son of man is glorified, and in him God is glorified; if God is glorified in him, God will also glorify him in himself, and glorify him at once. Little children, I am with you only a little longer. You will look for me; and as I said to the Jews so now I say to you, 'Where I am going you cannot come.' I give you a new commandment, that you love one another. Just as I have loved you, you also should love one another. By this everyone will know that you are my disciples, if you have love for one another.' Simon Peter said to him, 'Lord, where are you going?' Jesus answered, 'Where I am going you cannot follow me now; but you will follow afterward.' Peter said to him, 'Lord, why can I not follow you now? I will lay down my life for you.' Jesus answered, 'Will you lay down your life for me? Truly, truly, I say to you, before the cock crows, you will have denied me three times.'

John 13: 31–8

If you prefer to take a different Bible reading each day, there is a full list of suggested passages at the back of the book (pages 238–254). The readings for Holy Week are on page 244.

Pause for reflection

A Song of Lamentation

1 Is it nothing to you, all you who pass by?
   look and see if there is any sorrow like my sorrow.

2 For I weep, my eyes flow with tears:
   and a comforter is far from me, one to revive my
   courage.

3 My children are in desolation:
  and the enemy has prevailed.

4 Remember my affliction and my bitterness:
  the wormwood and the gall.

5 My soul continually thinks of it:
  and is bowed down within me.

6 But this I call to mind:
  and therefore I am hopeful,

7 That the Lord is kind to those who wait for him:
  to the soul that seeks him.

8 It is good that we should wait quietly:
  for the salvation of the Lord.

Lamentations 1: 12a, 16; 3: 19–21, 25–6

Glory to the Father, and to the Son:
    and to the Holy Spirit;
as it was in the beginning, is now:
    and shall be for ever. Amen.

OR

A Song of the Mystery of Christ's Self-giving

Now my tongue the mystery telling
    of the glorious body sing,
and the blood, all price excelling,
    which the Gentiles' Lord and King,
in a Virgin's womb once dwelling,
    shed for this world's ransoming.

That last night, at supper lying,
   'mid the Twelve, his chosen band,
Jesus, with the rites complying,
   keeps the feast as laws demand:
then, more precious food supplying,
   gives himself with his own hand.

Glory let us give and blessing
   to the Father and the Son,
honour, might and praise addressing,
   while eternal ages run;
ever too his love confessing,
   who, from both, with both is one.

St Thomas Aquinas (1225–74)

PRAYERS

Lord have mercy: in you I trust;
Christ have mercy: on you I depend;
Lord have mercy: you are my peace.

THE LORD'S PRAYER

I give thanks . . .

I confess . . .

I ask for help and guidance . . .

I pray for those I love . . .
       for people I encounter in my daily life . . .
       for those carrying responsibilities . . .
       for those in need or distress . . .

Thanks be to you, my Lord Jesus Christ,
    for all the benefits you have won for me,
    for all the pains and insults you have borne for me.
O most merciful Redeemer, Friend and Brother,
    may I know you more clearly,
    love you more dearly,
    and follow you more nearly,
    for ever and ever.

        St Richard of Chichester (1197–1253)

OR

Jesus, Lord of the Cross,
    I thank you
    that you went into the heart of our evil and pain,
    along a way that was both terrible and wonderful,
    as your kingship became your brokenness
    and your dying became love's triumph.

Conclusion

I bow down before the cross
in wonder and sorrow.
Holy God,
holy and strong,
holy and immortal,
have mercy on us. Amen.

A QUIET SPACE

Some suggestions for meditation and other ways of praying

Before you start

Spend some time being still and resting in God's presence. As a help, to lead you into quietness:

– sit comfortably with your back fairly straight;
– release the tension in your neck and head, and then in all of your body;
– listen to the sounds around you, first the distant ones, then the nearer ones.

Wait quietly on God;
                trust him;
                              let yourself go into his hands.

You might like to say quietly to yourself the name 'Jesus' or 'Lord' or 'Abba, Father' with the rhythm of your breathing.

Be still, and know that I am God. (Psalm 46: 10)

*   *   *

You will not necessarily find all the following ideas helpful. Use the ones that are right for you. But having chosen a meditation or passage, it is probably best to stick to it, rather than chopping and changing.

Holy Week

1. Prayerful reading

Take today's short Scripture passage under *A Thread for the Day,* or all or part of the longer reading in the suggestions for the year on page 244, and follow the way known as *Lectio Divina,* literally 'Divine' or 'Spiritual Reading' – see Appendix B on page 264.

* * *

2. To ponder

There was a scaffold in a courtyard of our prison in Dachau concentration camp. I used to look at it every day to receive its sermon. I had to pray a good many times because of it. It was not that I was afraid of being hanged on its scaffold one fine morning – one gets used even to this prospect as we all get used to the idea of having to die one day. No, what scared me was what I would do at the crucial moment. Would I cry out with my last breath, 'You are making me die like a criminal but you Nazis are the real criminals. There's a God in heaven and one day he'll prove it to you'?

If Christ had died like that, there would never have been a Gospel of the cross. No forgiveness, no salvation, no hope. There would have been no reconciliation on God's part; the Son of Man would never have been the Son of God. There would have been no new humanity bearing the very image of God himself.

If I were to die like that, even in the name of Christ, I would die an unbeliever, not believing that the prayer Jesus prayed on the cross was meant for me too. For none of us can live by the grace of God, or be fully reconciled with him, unless, at the same time, we offer mercy and forgiveness to our fellow human beings.

Martin Niemöller

I gaze on you, crucified Christ, in wonder and sorrow. Have mercy on me, a sinner, and help me to forgive all who have wronged me.

I ponder the awesome mystery of your passion, Lord, and I place my wounds in yours.

* * *

3. An imaginative exercise

Imagine that you are among the disciples and friends travelling with Jesus to Jerusalem, sensing that disaster is looming.

- Mingle with the crowds on Palm Sunday (Mark 11: 1–10) and watch Jesus riding along. What do you do? How do you feel? What does this mean to you?
- *On another day:* Share in the Last Supper with Jesus. Picture the scene, with oil lamps all round and everyone reclining around a low table. What is the atmosphere? How do you react when Jesus says, 'This is my body,' and 'This is my blood'? What strikes you most about Jesus now?
- *On another day:* Stand alongside Mary, Jesus' mother, at the foot of the cross. Stay there, as an act of love.

You may find it helpful to write down what happened during these exercises, and, at some point, to talk about it with a friend or spiritual director.

* * *

4. Reflect on Jesus' cup of suffering

On the way to Jerusalem Jesus said to the disciples, *'Are you able to drink the cup that I drink?' (Mark 10: 38)*

In the Garden of Gethsemane he prayed, *'Father, take this cup away from me; nevertheless, not my will but yours be done.' (Luke 22: 42)*

When Peter cut off the ear of the high priest's slave, Jesus said, *'Put away your sword; shall I not drink the cup which the Father has given me?' (John 18: 11)*

'Let this cup pass from me', he says, 'yet not as I will, but as you will.' The cup of which he was speaking was the cup into which the Holy Innocent One had drawn all the evils and poisons from all the world and which he was now being asked to drink to the dregs, so that through him no drop of evil, whether from the past or the present or the future, should remain beyond redemption.

Donald Nicholl

United with us in being and in love, Christ took on himself all the hatred, rebellion, derision, despair – 'My God, my God, why hast thou forsaken me?' – all the murders, all the suicides, all the tortures, all the agonies of all humanity throughout all time and all space. In all these Christ bled, suffered, cried out in anguish and desolation. But, as he suffered in a human way, so he was trustful in a human way: 'Father, into thy hands I commit my spirit.' At that moment death is swallowed up in life, the abyss of hatred is lost in the bottomless depths of love. A few drops of blood falling into the earth as into an immense chalice, have renewed the universe.

Olivier Clément

Christ, pouring yourself out,
love drained to the last drop,
I adore you.

Christ, kneeling as a servant, washing the disciples' feet,
shocking in your humility,
I adore you.

Christ, taking bread and wine,
crystal-clear in your awareness of the work you must
    complete,
I adore you.

Christ, entering Gethsemane, falling on your face to pray,
uncontainable in your broken heart,
I adore you.

*　　*　　*

NIGHT-TIME BLESSING

May the cross of our Lord
protect those who belong to Jesus,
and strengthen our hearts in faith,
in hardship and in ease,
in life and in death,
now and for ever.

Simon, Bishop of Iran (d. 339)

Easter

EASTER

Easter Day to the Eve of Ascension Day

The great fifty days between Jesus' resurrection and the sending of the Holy Spirit at Pentecost form a traditional time of celebration in the church. In 'Woven into Prayer' this period is divided into the two seasons of Easter and Ascensiontide. Easter is as important a season as Lent, with its mood of rejoicing in contrast to the sombre days which preceded it. It is a pity if we lose sight of this sense of thankfulness too soon after Easter Day itself.

A THREAD FOR THE DAY

Sunday

Jesus came and stood among the disciples and said, 'Peace be with you.'

John 20: 19b

Monday

Christ has been raised from the dead, the first fruits of those who have fallen asleep. For as by a man came death, by a man has come also the resurrection of the dead. For as in Adam all die, so also in Christ shall all be made alive.

1 Corinthians 15: 20–2

Tuesday

Jesus said to Simon Peter, 'Simon, son of John, do you love me?' He said to him, 'Yes, Lord; you know that I love you.'

From John 21: 16

Wednesday

At that same hour the two disciples rose from table and returned from Emmaus to Jerusalem; and they found the eleven and their companions gathered together. They were saying, 'The Lord has risen indeed, and he has appeared to Simon!' Then they told what had happened on the road, and how he had been made known to them in the breaking of the bread.

Luke 24: 33–5

Thursday

Moses said, 'I have set before you life and death, blessing and curse; therefore choose life, that you and your descendants may live, loving the Lord your God, obeying his voice, and holding fast to him.'

Deuteronomy 30: 19b–20a

Friday

'For the mountains may depart and the hills be shaken, but my steadfast love will never leave you, and my covenant of peace shall never be removed,' says the Lord, who has compassion on you.

Isaiah 54: 10

Saturday

Jesus said, 'In the world you will have trouble; but be of good cheer, I have overcome the world.'

John 16: 33b

A SHORT ORDER OF DAILY PRAYER

A moment of quiet: be still and know that God is here.

Begin with today's short piece of Scripture, under **A Thread for the Day**, *and reflect on that for a moment.*

Lord, touch my lips:
    that I may sing your praise with all my heart.

I greet you, risen Lord! Alleluia!
    You have conquered sin and death! Alleluia!

Glory to God, Father, Son and Holy Spirit:
    mystery of love, behind, through and beyond all things.

Rejoice, heaven and earth! Exult, all creation!
    Jesus Christ is risen! Alleluia!

As I turn my face to you, O God,
let my worship be once more a new beginning:
cleanse my spirit in your mercy,
draw me ever deeper into your love,
and accept my offering of praise and prayer
on behalf of the world;
through Jesus Christ,
our Brother and our Saviour. Amen.

Verses from Psalm 118

1 The Lord is my strength and my song:
   he has become my salvation.

2 Glad songs of victory:
   are heard in the tents of the righteous.

3 'The right hand of the Lord has triumphed,
   the right hand of the Lord is exalted!'

4 I shall not die, but live:
   and recount the works of the Lord.

5 The Lord has disciplined me harshly:
   but he has not given me over to death.

6 Open to me the gates of righteousness:
   that I may enter and give thanks to the Lord.

7 The stone which the builders rejected:
   has become the chief cornerstone.

8 This is the Lord's doing:
   and it is marvellous in our eyes.

9 This is the day which the Lord has made:
   we will rejoice and be glad in it.

10 Blessèd is he who comes in the name of the Lord:
    we bless you from the house of the Lord.

11 The Lord is God and he has given us light:
    make the festal procession with branches,
       up to the horns of the altar!

12 O give thanks to the Lord for he is good:
his steadfast love endures for ever.

Praise to you, O Christ,
once rejected and despised,
but risen again in triumph:
forgive our foolishness and sin,
and make us witnesses to your saving power,
for your love's sake. Amen

OR

Psalm 23

1 The Lord is my shepherd:
therefore I shall lack nothing.

2 He makes me lie down in green pastures:
he leads me beside the still waters.

3 He restores my soul:
he leads me in the paths of righteousness for his name's
sake.

4 Yea, though I walk through the valley of the shadow of
death, I will fear no evil:
for you are with me, your rod and your staff comfort
me.

5 You prepare a table before me in the presence of my
enemies:
you anoint my head with oil, and my cup overflows.

6 Surely goodness and mercy will follow me all the days
    of my life:
  and I shall dwell in the house of the Lord for ever.

Risen Lord,
you have passed through the valley
of the shadow of death,
and triumphed over evil:
be my shepherd and guide,
that I may stay close to you all my life,
and dwell in your house for ever. Amen.

Other psalms suitable for **Easter** are numbers 2, 16, 18 (in two
halves), 33, 105 (in two halves), 114, 116, 126, 136, 150.

Or you may want to use a psalm with a particular theme, see
pages 235–237.

At the end of the psalm you could use one of the psalm prayers
above, or the Gloria:

Glory to the Father, and to the Son:
  and to the Holy Spirit;
as it was in the beginning, is now:
  and shall be for ever. Amen.

SCRIPTURE READING

When the Sabbath was over, Mary Magdalene, Mary the
mother of James, and Salome bought spices, so that they
might go and anoint him. And very early on the first day
of the week, when the sun had risen, they went to the
tomb. They had been saying to one another, 'Who will roll
away the stone for us from the entrance of the tomb?'

When they looked up, they saw that the stone, which was very large, had been rolled back. As they entered the tomb, they saw a young man, dressed in a white robe, sitting on the right side; and they were alarmed. But he said to them, 'Do not be alarmed; you are looking for Jesus of Nazareth who was crucified. He has been raised; he is not here. Look, there is the place where they laid him. But go, tell his disciples and Peter that he is going ahead of you to Galilee; there you will see him, just as he told you.' So they went out and fled from the tomb, for terror and amazement had seized them; and they said nothing to anyone, for they were afraid.

Mark 16: 1–8

OR

Listen, I will tell you a mystery. We shall not all die, but we shall all be changed, in a moment, in the twinkling of an eye, at the last trumpet. For the trumpet will sound, and the dead will be raised imperishable, and we shall be changed. For this perishable body must put on the imperishable, and this mortal body must put on immortality. Then the saying that is written will be fulfilled:

'Death is swallowed up in victory.
O death, where is your victory?
O death, where is your sting?'

The sting of death is sin, and the power of sin is the law. But thanks be to God, who gives us the victory through our Lord Jesus Christ. Therefore, my beloved, be steadfast, immovable, always excelling in the work of the Lord, because you know that in the Lord your labour is not in vain.

I Corinthians 15: 51–3, 54b–58

Daily Prayer

If you prefer to take a different Bible reading each day, there is a full list of suggested passages at the back of the book (pages 238–254). The readings for Easter are on pages 244–245.

Pause for reflection

The Exsultet

1 Rejoice, heavenly powers! Sing, choirs of angels!
   Exult, all creation around God's throne!

2 Jesus Christ, our King, is risen!
   Sound the trumpet of salvation!

3 Rejoice, O earth, in shining splendour,
   radiant in the brightness of your King!

4 Christ has conquered! Glory fills you!
   Darkness vanishes for ever!

5 At this sacred time all evil is dispelled,
   guilt is washed away, and peace restored.

6 So we are reconciled with God.
   Alleluia! Amen!

OR

A Song of Christ's Supremacy

1 Christ is the image of the unseen God:
      the first-born of all creation.

2 For in him were created all things in heaven and on
      earth:
      everything visible and invisible.

3 All things were made through him and for him:
　　he is before all things, and in him all things hold
　　　　together.

4 He is the head of the body, the church:
　　he is the beginning, the first-born from the dead.

5 For in him all the fullness of God was pleased to dwell:
　　and through him to reconcile all things to himself,

6 Whether on earth or in heaven:
　　making peace by his death on the cross.

From Colossians 1: 15–20

Glory to the Father, and to the Son:
　　and to the Holy Spirit;
as it was in the beginning, is now:
　　and shall be for ever. Amen.

PRAYERS

Lord have mercy: in you I trust;
Christ have mercy: on you I depend;
Lord have mercy: you are my peace.

THE LORD'S PRAYER

I give thanks . . .

I confess . . .

I ask for help and guidance . . .

Daily Prayer

I pray for those I love . . .

> for people I encounter in my daily life . . .
> for those carrying responsibilities . . .
> for those in need or distress . . .

Almighty Father,
who in your great mercy made glad the disciples
    with the sight of the risen Lord:
give us such knowledge of his presence with us,
that we may be strengthened and sustained
    by his risen life,
and serve you continually in righteousness and truth;
through Jesus Christ your Son our Lord. Amen.

The Christian Year, Calendar, Lectionary and Collects

OR

Love of Jesus, fill me,
Joy of Jesus, surprise me,
Peace of Jesus, flood me,
Light of Jesus, transform me,
Touch of Jesus, warm me,
Strength of Jesus, encourage me.
O Saviour, in your agony, forgive me,
in your wounds, hide me,
and in your risen life take me with you,
for love of you and of your world.

Conclusion

Alleluia! Christ is risen!
    He is risen indeed, Alleluia!

A QUIET SPACE

Some suggestions for meditation and other ways of praying

Before you start

Spend some time being still and resting in God's presence. As a help, to lead you into quietness:

- sit comfortably with your back fairly straight;
- release the tension in your neck and head, and then in all of your body;
- listen to the sounds around you, first the distant ones, then the nearer ones.

Wait quietly on God;
>   trust him;
>   let yourself go into his hands.

You might like to say quietly to yourself the name 'Jesus' or 'Lord' or 'Abba, Father' with the rhythm of your breathing.

Be still, and know that I am God. (Psalm 46: 10)

* * *

You will not necessarily find all the following ideas helpful. Use the ones that are right for you. But having chosen a meditation or passage, it is probably best to stick to it, rather than chopping and changing.

Quiet Space

1. Prayerful reading

Take today's short Scripture passage under *A Thread for the Day,* or all or part of the longer reading in the suggestions for the year on pages 244 to 245, and follow the way known as *Lectio Divina*, literally 'Divine' or 'Spiritual Reading' – see Appendix B on page 264.

* * *

2. Some imaginative exercises

- Go into the garden very early in the morning to anoint the body of Jesus. How do you feel as you find the stone rolled away and think that the body has been taken somewhere else, so that you cannot even perform this final act of love for Jesus? Then you see someone in the half-light of morning. It must be the gardener. Maybe he will know where Jesus' body is. Through your tears, you ask for his help. And you hear him speak *your* name . . . (cf. John 20: 1–18).

- Be Thomas with the disciples in the upper room. It is your turn to buy bread, so you go out nervously, afraid of being recognized and arrested, hurrying through the back alleyways to the market stalls. You buy the bread and return, only to find that the others have totally changed. They are full of joy and elation, and are saying that they have seen Jesus, alive and present with them. How do you feel? What do you say? . . . Seven days later, you still feel the odd one out. They have all had an experience you haven't had. Then, suddenly Jesus is there in front of you, gently speaking to you. How do you respond to him? (cf. John 20: 24–9).

- Suppose that you are with the disciples who have gone back to Galilee to fish after Jesus' death (cf. John 21:

1–19). Jesus is standing on the shore; he welcomes you and has cooked breakfast for you. You sit down and eat with him, and, as you do so, you tell him about the ways in which you feel you have denied him or let him down. He listens attentively, and then, for each one of the things you have mentioned, he says, 'Do you love me? . . . Do you love me?' . . . Make your own response to him.

- Go on a walk (literally!) and make it into an 'Emmaus walk' (cf. Luke 24: 13–32). As you go along, talk to Jesus about the things that are on your mind. How does he respond?

Risen Christ, you were with your disciples on the road, even when they did not know it. Remind me that you are with me too, through each day's journey.

You may find it helpful to write down what happened during these exercises, and, at some point, to talk about it with a friend or spiritual director.

* * *

3. The Easter Icon: The Harrowing of Hell

If you can get hold of one of these icons, spend some time with it. Like all icons, it has been painted with prayer and fasting, and is intended to be a window into the glory of God, drawing you into the divine presence.

In the Orthodox tradition, Jesus' resurrection is celebrated as the moment when Jesus conquers death and opens up to us the gates of eternal life. In the icon, Jesus descends into death and hell, trampling the gates of hell underfoot and crushing the powers of evil. He bears the cross in his hand as a banner of victory. Within the dark-

ness over which Jesus is standing, you can see various instruments of imprisonment, e.g. keys, locks, chains, and sometimes also the nails, hammers and pliers used in crucifixion. All these represent the tools of the enemy.

In a powerful gesture, Jesus, the second Adam, grasps the wrist of Adam (the Hebrew word means 'the human race'), releasing him from bondage to sin and despair into the light of new life. Eve is on the other side (usually in red, as the complement to Adam), awaiting her turn to be lifted up out of hell too. Like the angels in the Icon of Jesus' baptism (described in the Epiphany *Quiet Space*, pages 62–64), Eve's hands are covered by her garments as a gesture of reverence. There is a diagonal burst of light, coming from the illuminated mountain behind Jesus, flowing down through his swirling garments, and on to the clothes of Adam himself. Yet there is also a movement in the opposite direction as Adam is pulled powerfully upwards. The whole composition is designed to convey this simultaneous double movement.

Behind Jesus you will see the same round (or occasionally almond-shaped) disc as on the Icons of the Transfiguration. This symbolizes eternity, expanding as it becomes progressively lighter.

Watching the scene on the left are the kings David and Solomon, and, behind them, John the Baptist and Moses. On the other side the figures represent Old Testament prophets who had looked forward in hope to the coming of Christ.

Stay with the icon and wonder at the mystery of Christ's descent into hell, the way his light penetrates the world of darkness and evil, and the freedom he offers us through his redeeming love, all so dynamically portrayed here.

He is the one who was not abandoned to hell, nor did his flesh see corruption. (Acts 2: 31)

Wake up, O sleeper, rise from the dead, and Christ will shine upon you. (Ephesians 5: 14b)

He has called you out of darkness into his marvellous light. (Based on 1 Peter 2: 9b)

* * *

4. Thanksgiving

Look over the events of the past few days and weeks, and focus on the good things: problems that were sorted out, lessons that you learned through mistakes, conflicts that ended in reconciliation; also the moments of happiness, laughter and delight.

Give thanks for these glimpses of resurrection power at work in our lives.

Glory be to you, radiant, risen Christ! Nothing can overcome the divine light and love that you have brought into our world. All praise to you!

*   *   *

NIGHT-TIME BLESSING

The blessing of God, the eternal goodwill of God, the shalom of God, the wildness and the warmth of God, be among us and between us, now and always. Amen.

Jim Cotter

Ascensiontide

ASCENSIONTIDE

Ascension Day to the Eve of Pentecost

In this book I have made Ascensiontide into a season in its own right, to restore to it its rightful significance. It is the season when we remember the necessity for the disciples to let go of Jesus, so that he can be present to all people at all times. We also celebrate the kingship of Christ, since his ascension into heaven is seen as the supreme moment when this is confirmed.

A THREAD FOR THE DAY

Ascension Day, and Tuesday of Week 2

If, then, you have been raised with Christ, seek the things that are above, where Christ is seated at the right hand of God. Set your minds on things that are above, not on things that are on earth. For you have died, and your life is hidden with Christ in God.

Colossians 3: 1–3

Friday in Week 1, and Wednesday in Week 2

Since we have a great high priest who has passed through the heavens, Jesus, the Son of God, let us hold fast to our confession of faith. For we do not have a high priest unable to sympathize with our weaknesses, but one who was tempted in every way as we are, yet without sin. Let us then approach with confidence the throne of grace, to receive mercy and find grace to help in time of need.

Hebrews 4: 14–16

Saturday, and Thursday of Week 2

I saw visions in the night, and behold, with the clouds of heaven there came one like a son of man; he came to the Ancient of Days and was presented before him. And he was given power and glory, that all nations and languages should serve him; his kingdom is an everlasting kingdom, that shall never be destroyed.

Daniel 7: 13–14a

Sunday, and Friday of Week 2

Then I saw a new heaven and a new earth; for the first heaven and the first earth had passed away. And the One who sat upon the throne said, 'Behold, I make all things new. I am the Alpha and the Omega, the beginning and the end.'

From Revelation 21: 1, 5–6

Monday, and Saturday of Week 2

As the disciples were looking on, Jesus was lifted up, and a cloud took him out of their sight. And while they were gazing into heaven, two men stood by them in white robes and said, 'Men of Galilee, why do you stand looking into heaven? This Jesus, who was taken up from you, will come in the same way as you saw him go.'

From Acts: 1: 9–11

A SHORT ORDER OF DAILY PRAYER

A moment of quiet: be still and know that God is here.

Begin with today's short piece of Scripture, under
A Thread for the Day, and reflect on that for a moment.

Lord, touch my lips:
    that I may sing your praise with all my heart.

Risen and ascended Lord, I worship you:
    Christ the King, I praise you.

Glory to God, Father, Son and Holy Spirit:
    mystery of love, behind, through and beyond all things.

I will worship the Lord:
    all praise to his name.

As I turn my face to you, O God,
let my worship be once more a new beginning:
cleanse my spirit in your mercy,
draw me ever deeper into your love,
and accept my offering of praise and prayer
on behalf of the world;
through Jesus Christ,
our Brother and our Saviour. Amen.

Psalm 113

1 Praise the Lord! Sing praises, you servants of the Lord:
   O praise the name of the Lord!

2 Blessèd be the name of the Lord:
   from this time forth and for evermore.

3 From the rising of the sun to its setting:
   let the name of the Lord be praised.

4 The Lord is high above all nations:
   and his glory is above the heavens.

5 Who is like the Lord our God who is enthroned on high:
   yet stoops down to look at the heavens and the earth?

6 He raises the lowly from the dust:
   and lifts the poor out of the dunghill.

7 He sets them among princes:
   even the princes of his people.

8 He gives the barren woman a home:
   and makes her the joyful mother of children.
      Praise the Lord!

Praise to you, glorious Lord,
for you have shared our human lot
and raised us up with you to heaven;
lift us out of darkness and despair,
and teach us to trust you always,
for your love's sake. Amen.

OR

Psalm 24: 1–8, 10b

1 The earth is the Lord's and all that is in it:
    the world and those who dwell therein.

2 For he has founded it upon the seas:
    and established it upon the waters.

3 Who shall ascend the hill of the Lord:
    and who shall stand in his holy place?

4 Those who have clean hands and a pure heart:
    who have not made a pledge to falsehood
    or made their oaths deceitfully.

5 They will receive a blessing from the Lord:
    and vindication from the God of their salvation.

6 Such is the generation of those who seek him:
    who seek the face of the God of Jacob.

7 Lift up your heads, O gates,
    and be lifted up, O everlasting doors:
    that the King of glory may come in.

8 Who is the King of glory?
    the Lord, strong and mighty, the Lord of hosts,
    he is the King of glory.

Creator God,
as we celebrate the rising up of your Son
out of the tomb and into the heavens,
cleanse and purify us
by his coming into our lives
as the true King of glory,
now and for evermore. Amen.

Other psalms suitable for **Ascensiontide** are numbers 2, 47, 99, 123.

Or you may want to use a psalm with a particular theme, see pages 235–237.

At the end of the psalm you could use one of the psalm prayers above, or the Gloria:

Glory to the Father, and to the Son:
   and to the Holy Spirit;
as it was in the beginning, is now:
   and shall be for ever. Amen.

SCRIPTURE READING

Jesus opened their minds to understand the scriptures, and he said to them, 'Thus it is written, that the Messiah is to suffer and to rise from the dead on the third day, and that repentance and forgiveness of sins is to be proclaimed in his name to all nations, beginning from Jerusalem. You are witnesses of these things. And see, I am sending upon you what my Father promised; so stay here in the city, until you have been clothed with power from on high.' Then he led them out as far as Bethany, and, lifting up his hands, he blessed them. While he was blessing them, he withdrew from them and was carried up into heaven. And they worshipped him, and returned to Jerusalem with great joy; and they were continually in the temple blessing God.

Luke 24: 45–53

OR

I pray that the God of our Lord Jesus Christ, the Father of glory, may give you a spirit of wisdom and revelation as you come to know him, so that, with the eyes of your heart enlightened, you may know what is the hope to which he has called you, what are the riches of his glorious inheritance among the saints, and what is the immeasurable greatness of his power for us who believe, according to the working of his great power. God put this power to work in Christ when he raised him from the dead and seated him at his right hand in the heavenly places, far above all rule and authority and power and dominion, and above every name that is named, not only in this age but also in the age to come. And he has put all things under his feet and has made him the head over all things and of the church, which is his body, the fullness of him who fills all in all.

Ephesians 1: 17–23

If you prefer to take a different Bible reading each day, there is a full list of suggested passages at the back of the book (pages 238–254). The readings for Ascensiontide are on pages 245–246.

Pause for reflection

A Song of Christ's Glory

1 Christ Jesus was in the form of God:
    yet he did not cling to equality with God.

2 He emptied himself, taking the form of a servant:
    and was born in human likeness.

3 Being found in human form he humbled himself:
    and became obedient unto death, even death on a
        cross.

4 Therefore God has highly exalted him:
    and given him the name which is above every name,

5 That at the name of Jesus every knee should bow:
    in heaven and on earth and under the earth,

6 And every tongue confess that Jesus Christ is Lord:
    to the glory of God the Father.

Philippians 2: 5b–11

Glory to the Father, and to the Son:
    and to the Holy Spirit;
as it was in the beginning, is now:
    and shall be for ever. Amen.

O R

A Song of the Revelation of Jesus

1 Jesus was made visible in the flesh:
    and vindicated by the Spirit.

2 He was seen by angels:
    and proclaimed among the nations.

3 He was believed in by the world:
    and taken up into glory.

4 He will be revealed at the due time:
    by God, the blessed and only Sovereign,

5 The King of kings and Lord of lords:
    who alone is immortal,

6 Who dwells in unapproachable light:
    whom no one has ever seen or can see.

7 To him be honour and everlasting power:
    for ever and ever. Amen.

1 Timothy 3: 16b; 6: 15–16

Glory to the Father, and to the Son:
    and to the Holy Spirit;
as it was in the beginning, is now:
    and shall be for ever. Amen.

PRAYERS

Lord have mercy: in you I trust;
Christ have mercy: on you I depend;
Lord have mercy: you are my peace.

THE LORD'S PRAYER

I give thanks . . .

I confess . . .

I ask for help and guidance . . .

I pray for those I love . . .
        for people I encounter in my daily life . . .
        for those carrying responsibilities . . .
        for those in need or distress . . .

Ascensiontide

Ascended Christ,
present at all times and in all places,
make me brave in following your way;
reign as king in my heart,
and, in the foolishness of the divine love,
free me from the ambitions
and power-games of worldly wisdom;
for your love's sake. Amen.

OR

Eternal God,
by raising Jesus from the dead
you proclaimed his victory,
and by his ascension
you declared him king.
Lift up our hearts to heaven
that we may live and reign with him.
Hear this prayer for your love's sake. Amen.

A New Zealand Prayer Book

Conclusion

I will bless the Lord. Alleluia! Alleluia!
    Praise to Christ the King! Alleluia! Alleluia!

A QUIET SPACE

Some suggestions for meditation and other ways of praying

Before you start

Spend some time being still and resting in God's presence. As a help, to lead you into quietness:

- sit comfortably with your back fairly straight;
- release the tension in your neck and head, and then in all of your body;
- listen to the sounds around you, first the distant ones, then the nearer ones.

Wait quietly on God;
> trust him;
>> let yourself go into his hands.

You might like to say quietly to yourself the name 'Jesus' or 'Lord' or 'Abba, Father' with the rhythm of your breathing.

Be still, and know that I am God. (Psalm 46: 10)

* * *

You will not necessarily find all the following ideas helpful. Use the ones that are right for you. But having chosen a meditation or passage, it is probably best to stick to it, rather than chopping and changing.

1. Prayerful reading

Take today's short Scripture passage under *A Thread for
the Day,* or all or part of the longer reading in the suggestions for the year on pages 245 to 246, and follow the way
known as *Lectio Divina,* literally 'Divine' or 'Spiritual
Reading' – see Appendix B on page 264.

*   *   *

2. To ponder

All his life long, Christ's love burnt towards the heart of
heaven in a bright fire, until he was wholly consumed in
it and went up in that fire to God.

Austin Farrar (1906–68)

To adore . . . that means to lose oneself in the unfathomable, to plunge into the inexhaustible, to offer
oneself to the fire and the transparency, and to give of
one's deepest to that whose depth has no end.

Pierre Teilhard de Chardin (1881–1955)

Christ, King of glory, I worship and adore you.

*   *   *

3. Letting go

The ascension of Jesus involves a huge adjustment for the
disciples. It is a new kind of bereavement, quite different
from the traumas of Calvary, but tough all the same.

They cannot hang on to Jesus; they have to let him go

once more, so that, in the eternal mystery of God, Christ can be present to us everywhere and at all times.

What Jesus did to rescue and restore many particular people whom he met during his lifetime in Galilee and Jerusalem, he now offers to do universally and for all. What he did for some particular people in healing and encouraging them, in reconciling and reuniting them with the power and the energy of God, he now offers to do for us and for all people. So we who were, like the Prodigal, in a far country of estrangement from ourselves and from God and from our neighbour, we too are brought home to the place where we belong.

John Bowker

For reflection:

- Is my God too small? Am I trying to hang on to an idea of him that is preventing me from growing in my faith?
- Loving always involves an element of letting go. We cannot grasp or hang on to the object of our love. Am I possessive about anyone I love?

Lord, I ask for courage and honesty, as I abandon myself to the unknown territory of faith. Help me to trust you, and to wait for you to 'clothe me with power from on high' in whatever way you know I need.

*   *   *

NIGHT-TIME BLESSING

While I sleep, O Lord,
let my heart not cease to worship you;
permeate my sleep with your presence,
while creation itself keeps watch,
singing psalms with the angels
and taking up my soul into its paean of praise.

Gregory Nazianzen (c. 330–90)

*This prayer picks up the theme found in the teaching of
some early Christian Fathers, that the whole of creation
offers to God an unceasing song of praise, in tune with the
worship of heaven. This continues while humans sleep,
and our souls may be taken up into this paean of praise at
any moment, sleeping or waking.*

Pentecost

PENTECOST

Whit Sunday to the 5th Saturday after Pentecost

In this book I am suggesting a season of Pentecost for a full five weeks after Whit Sunday, in order to give this important festival its due attention. As with Christmas and Easter, our celebration does not end immediately after the big day!

A THREAD FOR THE DAY

Sunday

Behold I will pour out my spirit on all flesh; your sons and your daughters shall prophesy, your old men shall dream dreams, and your young men shall see visions. Even upon your servants, in those days, I will pour out my spirit.

Joel 2: 28–9

Monday

I will sprinkle clean water upon you, and you shall be cleansed from all your uncleanness. A new heart I will give you, and a new spirit I will put within you; I will take out of you the heart of stone, and give you a heart of flesh. And I will put my spirit within you.

Ezekiel 36: 25a, 26–7a

Tuesday

Jesus said to the disciples, 'Peace be with you. As the Father has sent me, even so I send you.' And when he had said this, he breathed on them, saying, 'Receive the Holy Spirit.'

John 20: 21–2

Wednesday

Likewise the Spirit helps us in our weakness; for we do not know how to pray as we ought, but the Spirit himself intercedes for us with sighs too deep for words.

Romans 8: 26

Thursday

For just as there is one body, with many members, and all are members of the one body, so it is with Christ. For in the one Spirit we were all baptized into one body – Jews or Greeks, slaves or free – and we were all made to drink of the one Spirit.

1 Corinthians 12: 12–13

Friday

The wind blows where it wills; you hear the sound of it, but you do not know where it comes from or where it is going. So it is with everyone who is born of the Spirit.

John 3: 8

Saturday

Because you are his children, God has sent the Spirit of his
Son into your hearts, crying, 'Abba! Father!'

Galatians 4: 6

A SHORT ORDER OF DAILY PRAYER

A moment of quiet: be still and know that God is here.

Begin with today's short piece of Scripture, under
A Thread for the Day, and reflect on that for a moment.

Lord, touch my lips:
    that I may sing your praise with all my heart.

Spirit of flame, purify me:
    Spirit of freedom, empower me.

Glory to God, Father, Son and Holy Spirit:
    mystery of love, behind, through and beyond all things.

I will worship the Lord:
    all praise to his name.

As I turn my face to you, O God,
let my worship be once more a new beginning:
cleanse my spirit in your mercy,
draw me ever deeper into your love,
and accept my offering of praise and prayer
on behalf of the world;
through Jesus Christ,
our Brother and our Saviour. Amen.

Psalm 148: 1–13

1 Praise the Lord! Praise the Lord from the heavens:
  praise him in the heights!

2 Praise him, all his angels:
  praise him, all his host.

3 Praise him, sun and moon:
  praise him, all you shining stars.

4 Praise him, you highest heavens:
  and you waters above the heavens!

5 Let them praise the name of the Lord:
  for he commanded and they were created.

6 He established them for ever and ever:
  he set a law that cannot pass away.

7 Praise the Lord from the earth:
  you sea monsters and all deeps;

8 Fire and hail, snow and frost:
  stormy wind fulfilling his command.

9 Mountains and all hills:
  fruit trees and all cedars.

10 Wild beasts and all cattle:
  creeping things and birds that fly.

11 Kings of the earth and all peoples:
  princes and all rulers of the world.

12 Young men and maidens:
   old men and children.

13 Let them praise the name of the Lord:
   for his name alone is exalted,
      and his glory is above earth and heaven.

   Creator Spirit,
   in the beginning
   you moved over the face of the waters,
   and in the fullness of time
   you filled the apostles with joy.
   All praise to you, with the Father and the Son,
   one God, now and for ever. Amen.

OR

Psalm 27: 1–5, 7–8, 9b–12a, 14

1 The Lord is my light and my salvation; whom then
   shall I fear:
   the Lord is the stronghold of my life; of whom shall I
      be afraid?

2 When evildoers, even my enemies come upon me to
   devour me:
   they shall stumble and fall.

3 If an army should encamp against me my heart shall
   not be afraid:
   and if war should rise against me yet will I trust.

4 One thing I have asked of the Lord that I will seek:
   that I may dwell in the house of the Lord all the days
      of my life,

5 to behold the fair beauty of the Lord:
and to seek his will in his temple.

6 For he will hide me in his shelter in the day of trouble:
he will conceal me under the cover of his tent
and set me high upon a rock.

7 O Lord, hear my voice when I cry to you:
have mercy upon me and answer me.

8 You speak in my heart and say, 'Seek his face':
your face, Lord, will I seek.

9 For you have been my helper:
do not cast me away or forsake me.

10 Though my father and my mother forsake me:
the Lord will take me up.

11 Teach me your way, O Lord:
and lead me on a level path because of my enemies.

12 Do not deliver me into the hands of my adversaries:
for false witnesses have risen up, breathing out
violence against me.

13 O wait for the Lord, be strong, and let your heart take
courage:
wait for the Lord!

Faithful God,
my light, my strength and my salvation:
guide me along the way,
help me to trust you in times of trouble,
and fill me with your Spirit of peace,
now and all my days. Amen.

Other psalms suitable for **Pentecost** are numbers 8, 29, 84, 113, 114, 115, 117, 122, 146, 147.

Or you may want to use a psalm with a particular theme, see pages 235–237.

At the end of the psalm you could use one of the psalm prayers above, or the Gloria:

Glory to the Father, and to the Son:
   and to the Holy Spirit;
as it was in the beginning, is now:
   and shall be for ever. Amen.

SCRIPTURE READING

When the day of Pentecost had come, they were all together in one place. And suddenly from heaven there came a sound like the rush of a violent wind, and it filled the entire house where they were sitting. Divided tongues, as of fire, appeared among them, and a tongue rested on each of them. All of them were filled with the Holy Spirit and began to speak in other languages, as the Spirit gave them ability.

Acts 2: 1–4

O R

The fruit of the Spirit is love, joy, peace, patience, kindness, generosity, faithfulness, gentleness and self-control. There is no law against such things. And those who belong to Christ Jesus have crucified the flesh with its passions and desires. If we live by the Spirit, let us also be guided by the Spirit.

Galatians 5: 22b–24

Daily Prayer

If you prefer to take a different Bible reading each day, there is a full list of suggested passages at the back of the book (pages 238–254). The readings for Pentecost are on pages 246–247.

Pause for reflection

An Invocation of the Holy Spirit

Come, Holy Ghost, our souls inspire,
And lighten with celestial fire;
Thou the anointing Spirit art,
Who dost thy sevenfold gifts impart.

Thy blessèd unction from above
Is comfort, life and fire of love;
Enable with perpetual light
The dullness of our blinded sight.

Anoint and cheer our soilèd face
With the abundance of thy grace;
Keep far our foes, give peace at home;
Where thou art guide no ill can come.

Teach us to know the Father, Son,
And thee, of both, to be but One;
That through the ages all along
This may be our endless song:

Praise to thy eternal merit,
Father, Son and Holy Spirit.

Based on the Veni Creator Spiritus *(9th century)*

OR

St Patrick's Breastplate

I bind unto myself today
   the strong name of the Trinity,
by invocation of the same,
   the Three in One and One in Three.

Christ be with me, Christ within me,
   Christ behind me, Christ before me,
Christ beside me, Christ to win me,
   Christ to comfort and restore me.
Christ beneath me, Christ above me,
   Christ in quiet, Christ in danger,
Christ in hearts of all that love me,
   Christ in mouth of friend and stranger.

I bind unto myself today
   the strong name of the Trinity,
by invocation of the same,
   the Three in One and One in Three.
Of whom all nature hath creation,
   eternal Father, Spirit, Word;
praise to the Lord of my salvation,
   salvation is of Christ the Lord.

Based on the 'Lorica' or 'Breastplate Prayer'
ascribed to St Patrick (c. 389–c. 461)

PRAYERS

Lord have mercy: in you I trust;
Christ have mercy: on you I depend;
Lord have mercy: you are my peace.

THE LORD'S PRAYER

I give thanks . . .

I confess . . .

I ask for help and guidance . . .

I pray for those I love . . .
       for people I encounter in my daily life . . .
       for those carrying responsibilities . . .
       for those in need or distress . . .

Father of light, from whom every good gift comes,
send your Spirit into our lives
with the power of a mighty wind;
and by the flame of your wisdom
open the horizons of our minds.
Loosen our tongues to sing your praise
in words beyond the power of speech,
for without your Spirit
we could never raise our voices in words of peace
or announce the truth that Jesus is Lord,
who lives and reigns with you and the Holy Spirit,
one God, for ever and ever. Amen.

The Sunday Missal

OR

Almighty and all-loving God,
through the fire of your Spirit
you have drawn the hearts of men and women
to share in the mystery of your being;
by the power of the same Spirit
infuse our lives with your presence,
that, as your Son was transfigured in prayer,
we too may be transformed,
and our lives become a flame of self-giving love.

Conclusion

I will bless the Lord, Trinity of love:
now and for ever and unto ages of ages. Amen.

A QUIET SPACE

Some suggestions for meditation and other ways of praying

Before you start

Spend some time being still and resting in God's presence. As a help, to lead you into quietness:

– sit comfortably with your back fairly straight;
– release the tension in your neck and head, and then in all of your body;
– listen to the sounds around you, first the distant ones, then the nearer ones.

Wait quietly on God;
> trust him;
>> let yourself go into his hands.

You might like to say quietly to yourself the name 'Jesus' or 'Lord' or 'Abba, Father' with the rhythm of your breathing.

Be still, and know that I am God. (Psalm 46: 10)

* * *

You will not necessarily find all the following ideas helpful. Use the ones that are right for you. But having chosen a meditation or passage, it is probably best to stick to it, rather than chopping and changing.

1. Prayerful reading

Take today's short Scripture passage under *A Thread for the Day*, or all or part of the longer reading in the suggestions for the year on pages 246 to 247, and follow the way known as *Lectio Divina*, literally 'Divine' or 'Spiritual Reading' – see Appendix B on page 264.

* * *

2. Breathing prayer

On the first day of the week, Jesus came and stood among them saying, 'Peace be with you. As the Father has sent me, so I send you.' When he had said this, he breathed on them and said to them, 'Receive the Holy Spirit.' (cf. John 20: 21–2)

Lord, in this moment of quiet,
with the rhythm of my breathing:

>I breathe in your Spirit;
>I breathe in your peace;
>I breathe in your stillness;
>I breathe in your light.

Breathe on me, Spirit of Jesus, and help me to be aware of your calm presence throughout my life.

* * *

3. The Spirit praying in us

The Spirit helps us in our weakness; for we do not know how to pray as we ought, but the Spirit himself intercedes for us with sighs too deep for words. (Romans 8: 26)

Whenever we pray as Christians, we do not pray alone. We pray both through Christ and with Christ and in Christ, and Christ prays for us and with us and in us, so that, through the work of the Holy Spirit, our prayer becomes Christ's prayer and his prayer becomes our prayer. St Augustine reflects this understanding when he writes: 'When the body of the Son prays, it does not separate its Head from itself; and it is the one Saviour of his body, our Lord Jesus Christ, the Son of God, who prays for us, and prays in us, and he is prayed to by us. He prays for us as our priest; he prays in us as our head; he is prayed to by us as our God. Let us therefore recognise both our words in him and his words in us.'

Paul Bradshaw

Prayer is the energy of the Spirit, permeating, purifying and leavening a person, and, through that person, reaching out also to the cosmos.

André Louf

Let all my prayer be the prayer of the Spirit of Christ in and through me.

*   *   *

4. Fire of love

*Holy Spirit, fire of love, consume all that is rotten in me
and change me from the inside.*

*Holy Spirit, Comforter, melt all that is cold and
hard in me,
and soothe my hurts in your warmth.*

*Holy Spirit, transforming power, light up my heart
and take possession of me,
so that I may become flame.*

*   *   *

5. To ponder

The late Austin Farrar (1906–68) said of the Holy Spirit:

His action is like the rising water of the tide, ready to
fill every cranny that opens in the reef it engulfs, yet
forcing no openings that are not offered.

How does the Spirit of Christ shape our spirits? I am
going, in answer, to give you a very dull word – the
word is, *attitude*. The Christian who seeks in prayer and
sacrament the company of Christ, who puts himself into
the acts and concerns of Christ, is drawn quite without
consciousness, perhaps, into the attitudes of Christ. . . .
The attitudes are the basic things, the immediate form
of the divine life in us.

When we allow the love of God to move in us, we can
no longer distinguish ours and his. It is the firstfruits of
the Spirit.

Breathe in me, Holy Spirit,
that I may think what is holy.
Move me, Holy Spirit,
that I may do what is holy.
Attract me, Holy Spirit,
that I may love what is holy.
Strengthen me, Holy Spirit,
that I may guard what is holy.
Guard me, Holy Spirit,
that I may keep what is holy.

St Augustine of Hippo (354–430)

* * *

6. Reflection on the mystery of the Trinity

The Trinity is about what happens between us and God: Jesus taking us up into his own sonship, leading us into an intimate relationship with the Father, and opening to us the inexhaustible fountain of the Spirit.

The Father: God's being is a free and endless giving of life . . . reflecting and returning to its source.

The Son: Father and Son create together; but more than that. Their power is a power not only to give life, but to bring it to perfection to work within the world *in* our history.

The Spirit: That perfecting dimension of creative power is what we call 'Spirit'.

Rowan Williams

Pentecost

Living Love,
beginning and end,
giver of food and drink,
clothing and warmth,
love and hope:
life in all its goodness –
I praise and adore you.

Jesus, wisdom and word:
lover of outcasts,
friend of the poor;
one of us yet one with God;
crucified and risen:
life in the midst of death –
I praise and adore you.

Holy Spirit, storm and breath of love;
bridge-builder, eye-opener,
waker of the oppressed,
unseen and unexpected,
untameable energy of life –
I praise and adore you.

Holy Trinity, forever one,
whose nature is community;
source of all sharing,
in whom we love, and meet, and know our neighbour:
life in all its fullness,
making all things new:
I praise and adore you.

Brian Wren

* * *

7. An icon of the Trinity

If you can get hold of one of these icons, spend some time with it. Like all icons, it has been painted with prayer and fasting, and is intended to be a window into the glory of God, drawing you into the divine presence.

This icon celebrates the revelation of the central Christian doctrine of the Holy Trinity. It is a peaceful invitation to us to join in the scene, with several layers of symbolism and meaning. First there is the story in Genesis 18, when Abraham is visited by three mysterious figures. Abraham's hospitality has been interpreted from the earliest Christian centuries as an encounter with God, since the group of visitors is referred to as 'the Lord' in Genesis 18: 1 and 13. The three figures give a glimpse of the threeness of God, and so foreshadow the fuller revelation of the Trinity which comes through the New Testament.

In this icon, of which the most famous was painted by the Russian Andrei Rublev in 1425, there is a sense of harmony and a flowing, circular movement between each of the three persons of the Trinity. Their faces are the same, but there is also significant variation in the gestures of these angelic figures, suggesting unity within diversity, and the communion of mutual love. The movement begins with the right-hand figure, representing the Father, flowing to the Son in the centre, and, from the inclination of the head of the Son, to the Holy Spirit on the left – and so back to the Father. There is perpetual exchange and the communication of love, yet their gazes do not meet, so that there is a sense of space and freedom between them.

At the centre of the table is a dish, which some see as a chalice and others as a sacrificial lamb. Either way, it is a symbol of the suffering that Jesus accepts, and the fingers of the central figure of the Son here point to it as a way of acceptance. (On some icons there are a few other vessels as well.) Each figure holds a staff of authority.

Behind them we can see the oak tree at Mamre under which Abraham was sitting when the three arrived, and also his home, signifying the ordinary life into which the divine presence came.

The perspective is deliberately reversed (see the angle of the furniture beside the feet of the two front figures), so that, as we gaze at the icon, we are drawn into the calm fellowship of the table, and taken up into the gentle, loving movement at the heart of the Trinity.

Jesus prayed to the Father for his followers, 'As you are in me, and I in you, may they be in us. May they be one, even as we are one. I in them, and you in me . . . that the love with which you have loved me may be in them, and I in them.' (From John 17: 21–6)

* * *

NIGHT-TIME BLESSING

The blessing of the God of Sarah and of Abraham,
the blessing of the Son born of Mary,
the blessing of the Holy Spirit
who broods over us as a mother over her children,
be with us all. Amen.

Worship in an Indian Context

Ordinary Time 2

ORDINARY TIME 2

The 5th Sunday after Pentecost
(4th after Trinity) to 31 October

We now move on from the celebration of Pentecost and continue through the mid-year months until All Saints' Tide, Advent and Christmas. The number of weeks varies, depending on how early or late the date of Easter was. On 1 November (All Saints' Day) the season of All Saints' Tide begins.

A THREAD FOR THE DAY

Week 1

Sunday

Listen! I am standing at the door, knocking; if you hear my voice and open the door, I will come in to you and eat with you, and you with me.

Revelation 3: 20

Monday

The Lord said to Joshua, 'I will be with you; I will not fail you or forsake you. Be strong and of good courage.'

Joshua 1: 5b–6a

Tuesday

Whatever you do, in word or deed, do everything in the name of the Lord Jesus, giving thanks to the Father through him.

Colossians 3: 17

Wednesday

We can be reassured that, whenever our hearts condemn us, God is greater than our hearts, for he understands everything.

1 John 3: 19b–20

Thursday

The eternal God is your dwelling place, and underneath are the everlasting arms.

Deuteronomy 33: 27a

Friday

You are a chosen race, a royal priesthood, a holy nation, God's own people, so that you may proclaim the mighty acts of him who called you out of darkness into his marvellous light.

1 Peter 2: 9

Saturday

Encourage the fainthearted, care for the weak, be patient with all. See that none of you repays evil for evil, but always seek to do good to one another. Rejoice always; pray without ceasing, giving thanks in all circumstances.

1 Thessalonians 5: 14b–18a

Week 2

Sunday

'When Israel was a child, I loved him. It was I who taught Ephraim to walk, I took them up in my arms; but they did not know that I healed them. I led them with cords of compassion, with the bands of love. I became to them like one who lifts an infant to his cheek. I bent down and fed them,' says the Lord.

Hosea 11: 1a, 3–4

Monday

Yours, O Lord, is the greatness, the power, the glory, the victory and the majesty. For all that is in heaven and on earth is yours; yours is the kingdom, O Lord, and you are exalted as head above all.

1 Chronicles 29: 11

Tuesday

Trust in the Lord with all your heart, and do not rely on your own insight. In all your ways acknowledge him, and he will make your paths straight. It will be healing for your flesh and refreshment for your body.

Proverbs 3: 5–6, 8

Wednesday

In returning and in rest you shall be saved; in quietness and in trust shall be your strength.

Isaiah 30: 15b

Thursday

Now the Lord is the Spirit, and where the Spirit of the Lord is, there is freedom. And we all, with unveiled faces, beholding the glory of the Lord, are being changed into his likeness from one degree to another; this comes from the Lord, who is the Spirit.

2 Corinthians 3: 17–18

Friday

St Paul writes, 'For me, to live is Christ, and to die is gain. You have been granted the privilege, not only of believing in Christ, but also of suffering for his sake – sharing in the same conflict that you have heard I also faced and still do face.'

Philippians 1: 21, 29–30

Saturday

Finally, beloved, whatever is true, whatever is honourable, whatever is just, whatever is pure, whatever is pleasing, whatever is commendable, if there is any excellence and if there is anything worthy of praise, think about these things.

Philippians 4: 8

A SHORT ORDER OF DAILY PRAYER

A moment of quiet: be still and know that God is here.

Begin with today's short piece of Scripture, under **A Thread for the Day**, *and reflect on that for a moment.*

Lord, touch my lips:
  that I may sing your praise with all my heart.

O God make speed to save me:
  O Lord, come to my aid.

Glory to God, Father, Son and Holy Spirit:
  mystery of love, behind, through and beyond all things.

I will worship the Lord:
  all praise to his name.

As I turn my face to you, O God,
let my worship be once more a new beginning:
cleanse my spirit in your mercy,
draw me ever deeper into your love,
and accept my offering of praise and prayer
on behalf of the world;
through Jesus Christ,
our Brother and our Saviour. Amen.

Verses from Psalm 25

1 Unto you, O Lord, I lift up my soul:
  in you have I trusted, let me not be put to shame,
    nor let my enemies triumph over me.

2 Let not those who wait for you be put to shame:
  but let the treacherous be frustrated in their schemes.

3 Show me your ways, O Lord:
  and teach me your paths.

4 Lead me in your truth and guide me:
  for you are the God of my salvation;
    in you have I trusted all the day long.

5 Remember your mercy and compassion, O Lord:
  for they are from of old.

6 Do not remember the sins of my youth and my
    transgressions:
  but consider me according to your steadfast love.

7 Good and upright is the Lord:
  therefore he directs sinners in the way.

8 He guides the humble towards what is right:
  and teaches the meek his way.

9 My eyes are ever looking towards the Lord:
  for he will pluck my feet out of the net.

10 O guard my life and deliver me:
  let me not be put to shame, for I take refuge in you.

11 May integrity and uprightness preserve me:
for my hope is in you.

Lord Jesus Christ, grant me the grace
to live with humility, hope and integrity;
let my life be ruled
not by fear of what anyone can do to me,
but by delight in your will
and trust in your saving presence,
now and always. Amen.

OR

Psalm 42: 1–5

1 As a deer longs for flowing streams:
so longs my soul for you, O God.

2 My soul thirsts for God, yea for the living God:
when shall I come and behold his face?

3 My tears have been my food day and night:
while all day long they ask me, 'Where now is your
God?'

4 I pour out my soul when I remember these things:
how I went with the throng, and led them into the house
of God.

5 With glad shouts and songs of thanksgiving:
a multitude keeping high festival.

6 Why are you so full of heaviness, O my soul:
and why so disquieted within me?

7 O put your trust in God:
   for I shall praise him again,
      who is my helper and my God.

Loving God,
source and goal of my deepest desires,
help me when burdens weigh heavily,
and renew my soul with streams of living water,
that I may serve you with all my heart
in the strength of Jesus Christ my Lord. Amen.

During **Ordinary Time 2** *you may also want to use a psalm with*
a particular theme, see pages 235–237.

At the end of the psalm you could use one of the psalm prayers
above, or the Gloria:

Glory to the Father, and to the Son:
   and to the Holy Spirit;
as it was in the beginning, is now:
   and shall be for ever. Amen.

SCRIPTURE READING

Jesus said, 'Therefore I tell you, do not worry about your
life, what you will eat or what you will drink, or about
your body, what you will wear. Is not life more than food,
and the body more than clothing? Look at the birds of the
air; they neither sow nor reap nor gather into barns, and
yet your heavenly Father feeds them. Are you not of more
value than they? And can any of you by worrying add a
single hour to your span of life? And why do you worry
about clothing? Consider the lilies of the field, how they

grow; they neither toil nor spin, yet I tell you, even Solomon in all his glory was not clothed like one of these. But if God so clothes the grass of the field, which is alive today and tomorrow is thrown into the oven, will he not much more clothe you – you of little faith? But seek first the kingdom of God and his righteousness, and all these things will be given to you as well.'

Matthew 6: 25–30, 33

OR

Now the apostles and the believers who were in Judea heard that the Gentiles had also accepted the word of God. So when Peter went up to Jerusalem, the circumcised believers criticized him, saying, 'Why did you go to uncircumcised men and eat with them?' Then Peter began to explain it to them, step by step, saying, 'I was in the city of Joppa praying, and in a trance I saw a vision. There was something like a large sheet coming down from heaven, being lowered by its four corners; and it came close to me. As I looked at it closely I saw four-footed animals, beasts of prey, reptiles, and birds of the air. I also heard a voice saying to me, "Get up, Peter; kill and eat." But I replied, "By no means Lord; for nothing profane or unclean has ever entered my mouth." But a second time the voice answered from heaven, "What God has made clean, you must not call profane." This happened three times; then everything was pulled up again to heaven. At that very moment three men, sent to me from Caesarea, arrived at the house where we were. The Spirit told me to go with them and not to make a distinction between them and us. These six brothers also accompanied me, and we entered the man's house. He told us how he had seen the angel standing in his house and saying, "Send to Joppa and bring Simon, who is called Peter; he will give you a message by which you and your entire household will be saved." And as I began to speak, the Holy Spirit fell upon them just as it had upon us at the beginning. And I remembered the word of the Lord, how he had said, "John baptized with water, but you will be baptized with the Holy Spirit." If God gave them the same gift that he gave us when we believed in the Lord Jesus Christ, who was I that I could hinder God?' When they heard this, they were silenced. And they praised God, saying, 'Then God has given even to the Gentiles the repentance that leads to life.'

Acts 11: 1–18

If you prefer to take a different Bible reading each day, there is a full list of suggested passages at the back of the book (pages 238–254). The readings for Ordinary Time 2 are on pages 247–252.

Pause for reflection

Verses from the Benedicite

O you works of the Lord,
O you angels of the Lord,
O you heavens, bless the Lord!
Praise him and magnify him for ever!

O you sun and moon,
O you stars of heaven,
O you rain and dew, bless the Lord!
Praise him and magnify him for ever!

O you winds that blow,
O you fire and heat,
O you frost and snow, bless the Lord!
Praise him and magnify him for ever!

O let the whole earth
and the souls of the righteous
and the people of God, bless the Lord!
Let us praise him and magnify him for ever!

OR

A Song of Praise

Greetings to God the Father
        present in all the earth,
        and in the heavens,
        and beyond the heavens.
Greetings to the Son, Lord of hope,
        rising like the dawn in our hearts.
Greetings to the Spirit, power of flame,
        giver of peace.
        May your peace and power
        be diffused and known
        among all people.
And may the love of the saints
        and the glory of the angels
        inspire us in your church
        and fill us with unquenchable hope.

Source unknown

PRAYERS

Lord have mercy: in you I trust;
Christ have mercy: on you I depend;
Lord have mercy: you are my peace.

THE LORD'S PRAYER

I give thanks . . .

I confess . . .

I ask for help and guidance . . .

I pray for those I love . . .
  for people I encounter in my daily life . . .
  for those carrying responsibilities . . .
  for those in need or distress . . .

Almighty God, you have made us for yourself, and our hearts are restless till they find rest in you. Grant us purity of heart and strength of purpose, that no selfish passion may hinder us from knowing your will, and no weakness hinder us from doing it; but that in your light we may see light, and in your service find our perfect freedom; through Jesus Christ our Lord.

St Augustine of Hippo (354–430)

OR

Jesus, Son of God,
let your love shine through our eyes,
your Spirit inspire our words,
your wisdom fill our minds,
your mercy control our hands,
your will capture our hearts,
your joy pervade our being;
until we are changed into your likeness
from glory to glory.

Michael Perry

Conclusion

I will bless the Lord.
   Thanks be to God.

A QUIET SPACE

Some suggestions for meditation and other ways of praying

Before you start

Spend some time being still and resting in God's presence. As a help, to lead you into quietness:

- sit comfortably with your back fairly straight;
- release the tension in your neck and head, and then in all of your body;
- listen to the sounds around you, first the distant ones, then the nearer ones.

Wait quietly on God;
>   trust him;
>   let yourself go into his hands.

You might like to say quietly to yourself the name 'Jesus' or 'Lord' or 'Abba, Father' with the rhythm of your breathing.

Be still, and know that I am God. (Psalm 46: 10)

* * *

You will not necessarily find all the following ideas helpful. Use the ones that are right for you. But having chosen a meditation or passage, it is probably best to stick to it, rather than chopping and changing.

Quiet Space

1. Prayerful reading

Take today's short Scripture passage under *A Thread for the Day*, or all or part of the longer reading in the suggestions for the year on pages 247 to 252, and follow the way known as *Lectio Divina*, literally 'Divine' or 'Spiritual Reading' – see Appendix B on page 264.

* * *

2. Unmasked?!

When we pray we are both cherished and unmasked. Not unmasked in the sense of a brutal stripping, but gently and inexorably exposed to the pure, penetrating light of God.

When we open ourselves up to God, we find ourselves, like the Prodigal Son, surprised by the embrace of our loving Father. As we become more inwardly quiet and let go of the clamour in our brains, our pretences fall away and our false ideas about our own ego lose their power, so that we begin to discover our true selves, made in God's image.

Thus, each time we pray and focus our attention on God rather than on ourselves, we make a fresh start, and are loved a bit more into the person we were created to be.

Here I am, Lord.
I cannot fathom or hold you;
I can only ask you
to take hold of me.
I cannot grasp or contain you
in a formula or tradition;
I can only ask you to fill me with yourself,
and make me part
of the mystery of your presence
in the world.

3. A time of intercession

Which items in recent news bulletins have particularly struck you? Spend some time being with God *for* these people and situations.

Which people come to mind who are going through trouble or difficulty at the moment? Hold them silently in the outpouring love of God.

> Spirit of Christ,
> accept and transform
> my small energy of desire,
> that it may become
> part of your great energy of desire
> for the redemption of the world.
> Your will be done!

Evelyn Underhill (1875–1941)

* * *

4. An icon of the Transfiguration of Jesus

6 August is the day when the church remembers the Transfiguration.

If you can get hold of one of these icons, spend some time with it. Like all icons, it has been painted with prayer and fasting, and is intended to be a window into the glory of God, drawing you into the divine presence.

By tradition, this is the first scene to be painted by a newly trained icon-painter, as it sums up the essence of icon painting, i.e. the divine radiance shining through the world of matter. The material of the painter is wood and

paint, while the material of the Transfiguration is Jesus'
physical body.

See how the glory of the transfigured Christ is not
limited to the top part of the scene, but spreads to the
world around, and is reflected on the rocks (representing
all creation) and on the bodies of Peter, James and John.

The circular or almond-shaped disc behind Jesus, expanding as it becomes progressively lighter, is a symbol of eternity. Eternity intersects with time, as the figures of Moses and Elijah are seen talking with Jesus about the suffering he is to face. They represent the law and the prophets, whose message Jesus will bring to its fulfilment.

The disciples are prostrate, overwhelmed with amazement and fear, and shielding their eyes from the dazzling light. Peter is often shown as plucking up a bit more courage than the others in order to peep at the scene. On some icons we see the disciples' sandals flying off in a delightfully human detail.

There is a strong sense of balance and harmony, both in the design and the colours, which are warm, ranging from yellow ochre to red. Moses' garments are usually a similar colour to those of some of the disciples. The focal point is the figure of the transfigured Christ, in whom 'all the fullness of God was pleased to dwell' (Colossians 1: 19). The three figures in the heavenly dimension above are balanced by the three disciples below on earth. The meeting of heaven and earth is symbolized by the mountain which spreads downwards in a triangular shape to reach us all, so that we can share in the mystery of what is happening: *and we all, with unveiled face, beholding the glory of the Lord, are being changed into his likeness, from one degree of glory to another. (2 Corinthians 3: 18a)*

Lord, how good it is for us to be here. (from Luke 9: 33)

Heaven and earth, O Lord, are full of your glory
and all creation resounds with your praise.
As your Son has appeared in the likeness of our flesh

so may all creation share in the beauty of holiness;
through Jesus Christ our Lord. Amen.

Celebrating Common Prayer

To ponder

Jesus could have simply told them in a conversation or
teaching-session that he was the radiant, divine and
beloved Son of God, and that his sonship was intimately
bound up with going to Jerusalem to suffer, fulfilling all
that Moses and Elijah stood for. But if they were going to
understand this properly, it was necessary for Peter, James
and John to receive the overwhelming visual and aural
impact of what happened on the mountain. They needed
the glory and the cloud, the wonder and the fear, the
poetry and the mystery, the words and the silence, to
convey to them things that discourse alone could not
adequately express. Even then, it was still a matter of
knowing and not knowing, holding on to a faith deeper
than words.

The same probably applies to us.

*   *   *

5. Accepting our limitations

What are the unavoidable limitations I face in my life? Do
I try to resist or deny them?

The hardest thing is to accept not only the limitations of
the environment but the limitations in oneself. For a
time, while I am young, facing my limitations is not
imperative, because I can always tell myself that I have
not yet had time to achieve my dream. Given time, I
shall get there. But the day comes when I realise that I

am never going to achieve it, because I am not the sort of person who can. The ideal means as much to me as ever, but my instrument will not play that note. It is a very painful realisation, and much may depend on what I do with it. I can rebel and refuse to face it, which leads to resentment and a flirtation with unreality. I can acquiesce in a cynical and disillusioned way, which leads to loss of the vision and checks growth. Or I can accept it very lovingly in faith.

At a greater depth than before I am being asked to accept the reality of the human condition. God's Son accepted it in his incarnation more deeply and lovingly than I shall ever be able to, but my acceptance is within his. He did the Father's perfect work within his limited humanity, and all humanity's limitations are shot through with glory in consequence. God has chosen, freely chosen, to work creatively within my limitations too. When I accept them *I am consenting to go along with his vision*, not acquiescing in some kind of regretful decision on his part to make the best of a bad job.

Maria Boulding (my italics)

Lord, show me when and how to say Yes to my limitations.

* * *

6. An imaginative exercise

Choose one of the accounts of Jesus healing people in the Gospels. For example:

the leper (Mark 1: 40–5)
the paralysed man (Mark 2: 1–12)
Jairus' daughter (Mark 5: 21–4, 35–43)

the woman with a haemorrhage (Mark 5: 25–34)
blind Bartimaeus (Mark 10: 46–52).

- Which character in the story do you want to be?
- What do you say to Jesus?
- How does he respond to you?

You may find it helpful to write down what happened during these exercises, and, at some point, to talk about it with a friend or spiritual director.

* * *

7. What do I want?

Try to identify some of the things you want most in your life and in your relationship with God.

Make these into a prayer. Give to God your varied desires; remain quietly in his presence.

> It is not what you are, nor what you have been, that God takes account of with his all-merciful eyes, but what you *desire* to be.
>
> *The Cloud of Unknowing (14th century)*

My Lord God,
I have no idea where I am going,
I do not see the road ahead of me,
I cannot know for certain where it will end.

Nor do I really know myself;
and the fact that I think I am following your will
does not mean that I am actually doing so.

But I believe that the desire to please you
does in fact please you.
And I hope I have that desire in all that I am doing.

I hope that I will never do anything
apart from that desire to please you.

And I know that if I do this
you will lead me by the right road,
though I may know nothing about it.

Therefore I will trust you always,
though I may seem to be lost
and in the shadow of death.
I will not fear, for you are ever with me,
and you will never leave me to make my journey alone.

Thomas Merton

*   *   *

8. Pray with some incense (or an incense stick)

Incense was used in both Old Testament and New Testament times, as a sign of the offering of prayer and worship to God.

You shall make an altar upon which to burn incense; and Aaron shall burn fragrant incense on it. Every morning when he dresses the lamps he shall burn it, and when he sets up the lamps in the evening. (Exodus 30: 1a, 7–8a)

In Jesus' time there was an altar of incense in the Holy Place, a small building within the precincts of the Temple. Priests from miles around drew lots for the privilege of offering the day's evening incense on behalf of the people gathered outside. It was a significant moment when everyone saw the smoke rising up, a symbol of each person's prayer rising up to God.

It was while he was performing this duty of burning incense that John the Baptist's father, Zechariah, encountered the angel who told him that his wife would have a son (Luke 1: 5–25).

In one of the great visions in the Book of Revelation, we are told that an angel held a golden censer with 'a great quantity of incense', and that his offering of incense was mingled with the prayers of all the saints before the throne of God (cf. Revelation 8: 3-4). From the fifth century onwards, Christians made a morning and evening offering of incense as a regular practice, a sign of the constant flow of prayer offered to God by his people mingling with the prayers of those who were now in heaven. In the evenings they often said verses from Psalm 141 at the same time. You could use these words as a prayer now:

I call upon you, O Lord; make haste to help me!
Give ear to my voice when I call to you.
Let my prayer be counted as incense before you,
the lifting up of my hands as the evening sacrifice.

Psalm 141: 1–2

Pray for Christians throughout the world in whose offering of prayer and worship – with its great variety – we share.

* * *

9. To ponder

Transcript of a talk given on BBC Television in November 1993 by Jean Vanier. He has founded many 'L'Arche' and 'Faith and Light' communities, which welcome people with severe learning difficulties.

In L'Arche, and in all our communities, I have seen the immense pain that is in the hearts of people with disabilities, particularly in those who have been rejected. You can see it coming from their depression, their anger, their terrible screams of loneliness. Many of them have just been put aside and told, 'You're no good, you're not wanted, you are a misfit, we don't want you here.' So they have been put away. Or maybe their parents loved them very much at home, but then they couldn't cope, or fell sick or died, and then people were put into hospitals or institutions. Now some of these places do care well for people; but some do not – and then there is terrible pain and an empty heart, and the sense that nobody cares about you because you have been put on one side. This anguish is quickly transformed into guilt, in the depths of people's hearts, as they begin to believe that it is all somehow their fault.

What Christ offers them, through us, is the greatest gift possible. It is unconditional love. We say to them, as Christ does, 'You are valuable because you are *you*; you are loved because you are *you*. You do not have to be clever or rich or successful in order to earn this love; you are a unique and special person, a child of God, who loves you with a love that is stronger than all pain and evil.'

And remember that it is not only people with disabilities who need to hear this message. We all do, because we are *all* vulnerable and handicapped in some way or another. For anyone who feels broken or unwanted, this mystery of love is pure gold.

God our lover,
in whose arms we are held,
and by whose passion we are known:
require of us also that love
which is filled with longing,
delights in the truth,
and costs not less than everything,
through Jesus Christ, Amen.

Janet Morley

*   *   *

NIGHT-TIME BLESSING

May the song of your Spirit soothe me,
your gentle arms cradle me,
your tenderness ease my tiredness
and your welcome enfold my weariness,
this night and always.
Amen.

All Saints' Tide

ALL SAINTS' TIDE

1 November to the Eve of Advent Sunday

At this time of year we remember that we are part of the communion of saints stretching across time and space. Our prayers, whether offered alone or together, are caught up in the great outpouring of praise and worship of the whole people of God. The commemorations of All Saints, the Departed and Remembrance Day are all part of this time.

A THREAD FOR THE DAY

Sunday

After this I was in the Spirit, and, behold, there stood in heaven a throne, with one seated on the throne. Around the throne are four living creatures. Day and night without ceasing they sing, 'Holy, holy, holy is the Lord God Almighty, who was and is and is to come.'

Revelation 4: 2, 6, 8

Monday

The twenty-four elders fall before the one who is seated on the throne, casting down their crowns and singing, 'You are worthy, our Lord and God, to receive glory, honour and power; for you created all things, and by your will they have their being.'

Revelation 4: 10–11

Tuesday

There is one body and one Spirit, just as you were called to the one hope that belongs to your call; one Lord, one faith, one baptism, one God and Father of all, who is above all and through all and in all. But each of us was given grace according to the measure of Christ's gift, to equip the saints for the work of ministry, for the building up of the body of Christ.

Ephesians 4: 4–7, 12

Wednesday

Now faith is the assurance of things hoped for, the conviction of realities we do not see. It is for their faith that our ancestors were commended.

Hebrews 11: 1–2

Thursday

Bless the Lord, O you his angels, you mighty ones who do his work, hearkening to the voice of his word. Bless the Lord, all his hosts, his ministers that do his will. Bless the Lord, O my soul!

Psalm 103: 20–1, 22b

Thread for the Day

Friday

Then he showed me the river of the water of life, bright as crystal, flowing from the throne of God; also, on either side, the tree of life, yielding its fruit each month. And the leaves of the tree were for the healing of the nations.

From Revelation 22: 1–2

Saturday

The servants of God shall see his face, and his name shall be on their foreheads. And night shall be no more; they need no light or lamp or sun, for the Lord God will be their light, and they shall reign for ever and ever.

From Revelation 22: 3–5

A SHORT ORDER OF DAILY PRAYER

A moment of quiet: be still and know that God is here.

Begin with today's short piece of Scripture, under **A Thread for the Day**, *and reflect on that for a moment.*

Lord, touch my lips:
    that with the angels and saints I may sing your praise.

O God, make speed to save me:
    O Lord, come to my aid.

Glory to God, Father, Son and Holy Spirit:
    mystery of love, behind, through and beyond all things.

I will worship the Lord:
    holy is his name.

As I turn my face to you, O God,
let my worship be once more a new beginning:
cleanse my spirit in your mercy,
draw me ever deeper into your love,
and accept my offering of praise and prayer
on behalf of the world;
through Jesus Christ,
our Brother and our Saviour. Amen.

Psalm 34: 1–10

1 I will bless the Lord at all times:
   his praise shall always be in my mouth.

2 My soul glories in the Lord:
   let the humble hear and be glad.

3 O magnify the Lord with me:
   let us exalt his name together.

4 I sought the Lord, and he answered me:
   he delivered me from all my fears.

5 Look to him and let your face shine with joy:
   and you shall not be ashamed.

6 In my wretchedness I cried to the Lord and he heard
      me:
   he saved me from all my troubles.

7 The angel of the Lord encamps around those who fear
      him:
   and he delivers them in their need.

8 O taste and see that the Lord is good:
   happy are those who take refuge in him.

9 O fear the Lord, you who are his holy ones:
   for those who fear him lack nothing.

10 The young lions suffer want and hunger:
   but those who seek the Lord lack nothing good.

All Saints' Tide

We thank you, O steadfast God,
that you are always with us;
help us, in fellowship with your saints,
to trust you at all times,
in the power of Jesus Christ, our Lord. Amen.

OR

Verses from Psalm 90

1 Lord, you have been our refuge:
    in every generation.

2 Before the mountains were born
        or the earth and the world were brought into being:
    from age to age you are God.

3 You turn us back to dust, saying:
    'Return, you children of the earth.'

4 For a thousand years in your sight
        are like yesterday when it is past:
    or like one watch of the night.

5 You sweep us away like a dream:
    like fresh grass in the morning.

6 In the morning it is green and flourishes:
    but in the evening it dries up and withers.

7 Teach us to number our days:
    that we may apply our hearts to wisdom.

8 May the graciousness of the Lord our God be upon us:
    O prosper the work of our hands.

Daily Prayer

Gracious God,
for whom a thousand years are as a day,
and whose eternity
intersects with our times:
prosper the works of our hands,
and grant us, moment by moment,
a sense of your unfailing presence,
through Jesus Christ, our Lord. Amen.

Other psalms suitable for **All Saints' Tide** are numbers 96, 121, 145, 148.

Or you may want to use a psalm with a particular theme, see pages 235–237.

At the end of the psalm you could use one of the psalm prayers above, or the Gloria:

Glory to the Father, and to the Son:
    and to the Holy Spirit;
as it was in the beginning, is now:
    and shall be for ever. Amen.

SCRIPTURE READING

After this I looked, and there was a great multitude that no one could count, from every nation, from all tribes and peoples and languages, standing before the throne and before the Lamb, robed in white, with palm branches in their hands. They cried out in a loud voice, saying, 'Salvation belongs to our God who is seated on the throne, and to the Lamb!' And all the angels stood around the throne and around the elders and the four living creatures, and they fell on their faces before the throne and wor-shipped God, singing, 'Amen! Blessing and glory and wisdom and thanksgiving and honour and power and might be to our God for ever and ever! Amen.'

Revelation 7: 9–12

OR

Therefore, since we are surrounded by so great a cloud of witnesses, let us lay aside every weight and the sin that clings so closely. Let us run with perseverance the race that is set before us, looking to Jesus, the pioneer and perfecter of our faith, who for the joy that was set before him endured the cross, despising the shame, and is seated at the right hand of the throne of God.

Hebrews 12: 1–2

If you prefer to take a different Bible reading each day, there is a full list of suggested passages at the back of the book (pages 238–254). The readings for the All Saints' Tide are on pages 252–254.

Pause for reflection

The Beatitudes

Blessèd are the poor in spirit:
　　for theirs is the kingdom of heaven.

Blessèd are those who mourn:
　　for they shall be comforted.

Blessèd are the meek:
　　for they shall inherit the earth.

Blessèd are those who hunger and thirst to see right
    prevail:
  for they shall be satisfied.

Blessèd are the merciful:
  for they shall receive mercy.

Blessèd are the pure in heart:
  for they shall see God.

Blessèd are the peacemakers:
  for they shall be called the children of God.

Blessèd are those who are persecuted for righteousness'
    sake:
  for theirs is the kingdom of heaven.

Matthew 5: 3–10

O R

Verses from the Te Deum

1 We praise you, O God:
    we acclaim you as the Lord.

2 All creation worships you:
    the Father everlasting.

3 To you all angels, all the powers of heaven:
    the cherubim and seraphim, sing in endless praise,

4 Holy, holy, holy Lord, God of power and might:
    heaven and earth are full of your glory.

5 The glorious company of apostles praise you:
the noble fellowship of prophets praise you.

6 The white-robed army of martyrs praise you:
throughout the world, the holy Church acclaims you,

7 Father of majesty unbounded:
your true and only Son, worthy of all praise,
the Holy Spirit, advocate and guide.

8 You, Christ, are the King of glory:
the eternal Son of the Father.

9 When you took our flesh to set us free:
you humbly chose the virgin's womb.

10 You overcame the sting of death:
and opened the kingdom of heaven to all believers.

11 You are seated at God's right hand in glory:
we believe that you will come to be our judge.

12 Come then, Lord, and help your people,
bought with the price of your own blood:
and bring us with your saints
to glory everlasting.

PRAYERS

Lord have mercy: in you I trust;
Christ have mercy: on you I depend;
Lord have mercy: you are my peace.

THE LORD'S PRAYER

I give thanks . . .

I confess . . .

I ask for help and guidance . . .

I pray for those I love . . .
      for people I encounter in my daily life . . .
      for those carrying responsibilities . . .
      for those in need or distress . . .

We thank you, O God, for the saints of all ages; for those who kept the lamp of faith burning in times of darkness; for the great souls who saw visions of larger truth and dared to declare it; for the multitude of quiet and gracious people whose presence has purified and sanctified the world; and for those we knew and loved, who are now in the fuller light of life with you; through Jesus Christ our Lord, Amen. *Anon.*

OR

We praise and thank you, Holy Spirit of God,
for the men and women you have called to be saints;
from your first fallible, frightened friends
who followed you to Jerusalem,
through the centuries of discovery and growth,
people of every class and temperament
down to the present day.
Help us to be Christ's united body to heal and reconcile;
help us to share Christ's life with everyone. Amen.

A New Zealand Prayer Book

Conclusion

I will bless the Lord with the whole company of heaven:
all praise to God, now and for ever. Amen.

A QUIET SPACE

Some suggestions for meditation and other ways of praying

Before you start

Spend some time being still and resting in God's presence. As a help, to lead you into quietness:

- sit comfortably with your back fairly straight;
- release the tension in your neck and head, and then in all of your body;
- listen to the sounds around you, first the distant ones, then the nearer ones.

Wait quietly on God;
> trust him;
>> let yourself go into his hands.

You might like to say quietly to yourself the name 'Jesus' or 'Lord' or 'Abba, Father' with the rhythm of your breathing.

Be still, and know that I am God. (Psalm 46: 10)

* * *

You will not necessarily find all the following ideas helpful. Use the ones that are right for you. But having chosen a meditation or passage, it is probably best to stick to it, rather than chopping and changing.

All Saints' Tide

1. Prayerful reading

Take today's short Scripture passage under *A Thread for the Day,* or all or part of the longer reading in the suggestions for the year on pages 252 to 254, and follow the way known as *Lectio Divina,* literally 'Divine' or 'Spiritual Reading' – see Appendix B on page 264.

* * *

2. The communion of saints

Reflect upon these words by Maggie Ross, which express beautifully the mystery of the communion of saints:

> Sometimes when I bow before the glory of God . . . I see from the corner of my eye, as mirrors reflect into other mirrors, an infinite line of shimmering figures bowing with me. Sometimes I will see them *en masse*, as crowds are painted in early Byzantine art. Or sometimes I will see a lone shepherd or hermit, voice roughened by years of singing against wind and sun, wandering in solitude. . . .
>
> They sang, sing, through nights and days, heat and cold, in home and hearth, desert and monastery, leaning in the weariness of the small hours against a bed, a stone wall, a carved misericord; in dressing-gowns, in skins, in heavy wool, in jeans, in ornate great-schemas, perhaps singing, as I once did with a Cistercian friend, on the subway in New York at midnight. But now there is no day and night for them as they sing: their time-bound, time-hallowed music lingers with us, though we know there is no time, only motion and bending of space–time. Their density, their holiness, their heart-songs bend with us, bend the continuum, bend before the glory of God, with the glory of God. . . .

Along with the great cloud of witnesses, sing or say, or whisper, or just think:

Holy, holy, holy.

Next time you attend a Eucharist, reflect upon the fact that, whenever we say these words, we are connected with our brothers and sisters, and offer our praises to God with angels, saints, apostles and fellow-pilgrims from every age.

*   *   *

3. We are part of something bigger

The following verses are part of an evening hymn, but their message about the unceasing stream of praise is as powerful at the start of a day as at its end:

We thank thee that thy church unsleeping,
    While earth rolls onward into light,
Through all the world her watch is keeping,
    And rests not now by day or night.

As o'er each continent and island
    The dawn leads on another day,
The voice of prayer is never silent,
    Nor dies the strain of praise away.

Lord, I thank you that, when I pray, I am never alone.

I pray for Christians all over the world, especially in places where people suffer for their faith.

*   *   *

4. To ponder

When you enter an Orthodox church, it is quite obvious who is at the centre of the faith of those who worship there, because you see a huge, central picture or mosaic of Jesus. And then, all round, high and low and in every corner, there are icons of the saints, reminding you that you are part of the company of heaven. Whether we are in church, at home, at work, or out of doors, we are always surrounded by the 'great cloud of witnesses'; for them, as for us, Christ is at the heart of everything.

With the angels and saints I offer you my love, O Lord. My heart sings with the angels, and my spirit dances with the saints. Thank you that, even with my mundane life and fragmented prayer, I am still part of this infinite and eternal mystery.

* * *

5. Saints

Who is your favourite saint?

What is it about the person that draws you?

What does that person show you about God?

How can that person's example enable you to discover who *you* are, and what your potentials might be? (This is not about imitation, or trying to force ourselves into a heroic mould. It is more about encouragement, allowing ourselves to become a bit more the person we were created to be.)

* * *

NIGHT-TIME BLESSING

God keep us in the fellowship of his saints.
Christ protect us by the ministry of the angels.
The Spirit make us holy in God's service;
and the blessing of God almighty,
the Father, the Son and the Holy Spirit
be upon us and remain with us always.

Michael Perham

Psalms Listed under Themes

Those in **bold type** are printed out in full in
the Short Orders of Daily Prayer

Thanksgiving and Praise

30
33
34 (All Saints' Tide)
40
47
66
67
89: 1–18
92
93
95
96
98 (Christmas)
103 (Lent)
105: 1–22
105: 23–45
107: 1–16
107: 17–32
107: 33–43
111
113 (Ascension)
116 and 117
118: 1–13 (Easter)

118: 14–29 (Easter)
135
138 (Epiphany)
145
147
148 (Pentecost)
150

Praise for God's Creation

8
19
65
104: 1–23
104: 24–37

Trust in God

4
16
20
25 (Ordinary Time 2)
27 (Pentecost)

Psalms

17
22 (Holy Week)
31
36 (Ordinary Time 1)
41
42 (Ordinary Time 2)
43
46 (Christmas)
54
55 (Holy Week)
56
57
69: 1–15
69: 16–23, 31–8
70
77
80

88
102
109: 1–4, 20–30
130 (Advent)
140
143

Penitence

32
38
51 (Lent)
85
103 (Lent)

Suggested Readings

Passages in **bold type** correspond roughly with those
printed out for specific reasons in the Short Orders of
Daily Prayer

ADVENT

*Week beginning Advent Sunday (i.e. the Sunday between
27 November and 3 December)*

Monday	**Luke 12: 35–40**
Tuesday	Malachi 3: 1–5
Wednesday	Zechariah 2: 10–13
Thursday	Micah 4: 1–8
Friday	Isaiah 9: 1–7
Saturday	Isaiah 11: 1–9

Week beginning the Second Sunday of Advent

Monday	**Isaiah 35**
Tuesday	Isaiah 40: 1–11
Wednesday	Isaiah 40: 12–17, 27–31
Thursday	Isaiah 41: 8–13
Friday	Isaiah 42: 1–9
Saturday	Isaiah 43: 1–7

Week beginning the Third Sunday of Advent

Monday	Isaiah 49: 1–6
Tuesday	Isaiah 52: 7–12
Wednesday	Isaiah 55: 1–13
Thursday	Luke 1: 5–25
Friday	Luke 1: 26–38
Saturday	Luke 1: 39–66

Suggested Bible Readings

Week beginning the Fourth Sunday of Advent
Move on to the Christmas Season on Christmas Day,
which falls some time this week.

Monday	Luke 2: 1–7
Tuesday	Luke 2: 8–20
Wednesday	Luke 2: 21–4
Thursday	Matthew 1: 18–25
Friday	Matthew 2: 1–12 (*N.B. the 'Holy Innocents' reading will be on 28 December*)
Saturday	Matthew 2: 19–23

CHRISTMAS

Christmas Day	**John 1: 1–14**
Boxing Day *(St Stephen)*	Acts 7: 54–8: 1a
27 December *(St John the Evangelist)*	1 John 1: 1–4
28 December *(Holy Innocents)*	Matthew 2: 16–18, and 18: 10
29 December	*catching-up day, or read John 1 again*
30 December	**Micah 5: 2–4**
31 December *(New Year's Eve)*	Revelation 21: 1–8
1 January *(New Year's Day)*	Isaiah 43: 18–21
2 January	Titus 2: 11–15
3 January	1 John 4: 7–12
4 January	1 John 4: 13–21
5 January	1 John 5: 1–13

239

Suggested Bible Readings

EPIPHANY

6 January	Isaiah 49: 7–18
7 January	Isaiah 50: 4–9
8 January	**Isaiah 60: 1–7**
9 January	Isaiah 60: 8–11, 19–22
10 January	**Matthew 3: 13–17**
11 January	John 2: 1–11
12 January	*a gap for whenever Sunday falls this week*
13 January	Romans 3: 21–31
14 January	Romans 5: 1–11
15 January	Romans 5: 12–21
16 January	Romans 6: 1–11
17 January	Romans 7: 13–25
18 January	Romans 8: 18–30
19 January	Romans 8: 31–9
20 January	*a gap for whenever Sunday falls this week*
21 January	Philippians 1: 1–11
22 January	Philippians 1: 12–26
23 January	Philippians 3: 2–16
24 January	Colossians 1: 24–9
25 January	Colossians 3: 12–17
26 January	1 Thessalonians 5: 12–28
27 January	*a gap for whenever Sunday falls this week*
28 January	1 Timothy 1: 1–2, 12–17
29 January	2 Timothy 1: 1–14
30 January	2 Timothy 2: 1–13
31 January	2 Timothy 4: 1–8, 19–22
1 February	*a gap for whenever Sunday falls this week*
2 February *(Presentation of Jesus)*	Luke 2: 22–40

Suggested Bible Readings

ORDINARY TIME I

*On **Ash Wednesday** move on to **Lent***

	Year 1	Year 2
3 February	**Genesis 1: 1–19**	Genesis 37: 1–11
4 February	Genesis 1: 20–2: 4a	Genesis 37: 12–36
5 February	Genesis 2: 4b–17	Genesis 39
6 February	Genesis 2: 18–25	Genesis 40: 1–15
7 February	Genesis 3: 1–15	Genesis 40: 16–23
8 February	Genesis 3: 16–24	Genesis 41: 1–16
9 February	*a gap for whenever Sunday falls this week*	
10 February	Genesis 4	Genesis 41: 25–45
11 February	Genesis 6: 1–10	Genesis 41: 46–57
12 February	Genesis 6: 11–22	Genesis 42: 1–17
13 February	Genesis 7: 1–10	Genesis 42: 18–28
14 February	Genesis 7: 11–24	Genesis 42: 29–38
15 February	Genesis 8: 1–12	Genesis 43: 1–15
16 February	*a gap for whenever Sunday falls this week*	
17 February	Genesis 8: 13–22	Genesis 43: 16–34
18 February	Genesis 9: 1–17	Genesis 44: 1–17
19 February	Genesis 11: 1–9	Genesis 44: 18–34
20 February	Ruth 1	Genesis 45: 1–15
21 February	Ruth 2	Genesis 45: 16–28
22 February	Ruth 3	Genesis 46: 1–7
23 February	*a gap for whenever Sunday falls this week*	
24 February	Ruth 4	Genesis 46: 28–34
25 February	Jonah 1	Genesis 47: 1–12
26 February	Jonah 2	Genesis 49: 28–50: 14
27 February	Jonah 3–4	Genesis 50: 15–26

Suggested Bible Readings

Years 1 and 2

28 February	Hebrews 1: 1–9
1 March	Hebrews 4: 12–16
2 March	*a gap for whenever Sunday falls this week*
3 March	Hebrews 5: 1–10
4 March	Hebrews 10: 11–25
5 March	**Hebrews 11: 1–12**
6 March	Hebrews 11: 13–28
7 March	Hebrews 11: 29–40
8 March	Hebrews 13
9 March	*this is the latest possible date for Shrove Tuesday*

LENT

Ash Wednesday	**Isaiah 58: 6–9**
Thursday	**Luke 11: 33–42**

	Year 1	Year 2
Friday	Genesis 12: 1–9	Exodus 1
Saturday	Genesis 13: 2–18	Exodus 2

Week beginning the First Sunday of Lent

	Year 1	Year 2
Monday	Genesis 15: 1–6	Exodus 3: 1–15
Tuesday	Genesis 16	Exodus 4: 10–17
Wednesday	Genesis 18: 1–15	Exodus 12: 1–14
Thursday	Genesis 21: 1–21	Exodus 12: 21–8, 37–42
Friday	Genesis 22: 1–19	Exodus 13:17– 14: 14
Saturday	Genesis 24: 1–33, 50–67	Exodus 14: 15–31

Suggested Bible Readings

Week beginning the Second Sunday of Lent

	Year 1	Year 2
Monday	Genesis 25: 19–34	Exodus 16: 1–3, 9–21
Tuesday	Genesis 27: 1–29	Exodus 19: 1–6, 16–25
Wednesday	Genesis 27: 30–45	Exodus 20: 1–21
Thursday	Genesis 28: 1–5, 10–22	Exodus 33: 7–23
Friday	Genesis 32: 9–12, 22–32	Exodus 34: 1–10, 29–35
Saturday	Genesis 33: 1–17	Deuteronomy 6: 1–12

Week beginning the Third Sunday of Lent

Monday	Genesis 35: 1–15, 27–9	Joshua 1: 1–9

Years 1 and 2

Tuesday	1 Corinthians 1: 1–9
Wednesday	1 Corinthians 1: 10–17
Thursday	1 Corinthians 1: 18–31
Friday	1 Corinthians 3: 18–4: 5
Saturday	1 Corinthians 4: 6–13

Week beginning the Fourth Sunday of Lent

Monday	2 Corinthians 1: 1–11
Tuesday	2 Corinthians 3: 17–4: 6
Wednesday	2 Corinthians 4: 7–18
Thursday	2 Corinthians 5: 11–21
Friday	2 Corinthians 6: 1–13
Saturday	2 Corinthians 12: 1–10

Passion Sunday

Week beginning the Fifth Sunday of Lent

Monday	Luke 19: 28–40
Tuesday	Luke 19: 41–8
Wednesday	Luke 20: 9–18
Thursday	Luke 20: 19–26

Suggested Bible Readings

Friday   Luke 20: 27–40
Saturday   Luke 21: 1–4, 37–8 and 22: 1–6

HOLY WEEK

Palm Sunday   *[John 12: 1–19]*
Monday   John 12: 20–6
Tuesday   John 12: 27–36
Wednesday   **John 13: 1–20**
Maundy Thursday   **John 13: 21–38**
Good Friday   John 19: 23–30
Easter Eve   John 19: 31–42

EASTER

Easter Day   *[Matthew 28: 1–10]*
Easter Monday   **Mark 16: 1–8**
Tuesday   John 20: 1–18
Wednesday   John 20: 19–31
Thursday   John 21: 1–8
Friday   John 21: 9–19
Saturday   John 21: 20–5

Week beginning the Second Sunday of Easter
Monday   Luke 24: 13–27
Tuesday   Luke 24: 28–35
Wednesday   Luke 24: 36–43
Thursday   1 Corinthians 15: 1–11
Friday   1 Corinthians 15: 12–19
Saturday   1 Corinthians 15: 20–8

Week beginning the Third Sunday of Easter
Monday   **1 Corinthians 15: 51–8**
Tuesday   John 8: 12–20

Suggested Bible Readings

Wednesday	John 8: 21–30
Thursday	John 8: 48–59
Friday	John 9: 1–17
Saturday	John 9: 24–41

Week beginning the Fourth Sunday of Easter

Monday	John 10: 1–18
Tuesday	John 11: 1–16
Wednesday	John 11: 17–27
Thursday	John 11: 28–44
Friday	John 14: 1–11
Saturday	John 14: 12–24

Week beginning the Fifth Sunday of Easter

Monday	John 14: 25–31
Tuesday	John 15: 1–11
Wednesday	John 15: 12–17
Thursday	John 15: 18–27
Friday	John 16: 1–15
Saturday	John 16: 16–24

Week beginning the Sixth Sunday of Easter

Monday	John 16: 25–33
Tuesday	John 17: 1–11
Wednesday	John 17: 12–26

Ascension Day (move on to the next season)

ASCENSIONTIDE

Ascension Day	**Luke 24: 45–53**
Friday	Ephesians 1: 1–14
Saturday	**Ephesians 1: 15–23**

Suggested Bible Readings

**Week beginning the Sunday after Ascension Day
(also called the Seventh Sunday of Easter)**

Monday	Ephesians 2: 1–10
Tuesday	Ephesians 2: 11–22
Wednesday	Ephesians 3: 1–13
Thursday	Ephesians 3: 14–21
Friday	Ephesians 4: 1–16
Saturday	Ephesians 6: 10–24

PENTECOST

Week beginning WHIT SUNDAY (Day of Pentecost)

Monday	**Acts 2: 1–13**
Tuesday	**Galatians 5: 22–6**
Wednesday	Isaiah 61: 1–4
Thursday	Ezekiel 36: 24–8
Friday	Ezekiel 37: 1–14
Saturday	Romans 8: 1–8

Week beginning TRINITY SUNDAY

Monday	Isaiah 6: 1–8
Tuesday	Romans 8: 18–30
Wednesday	Romans 8: 31–39
Thursday	1 Corinthians 11: 23–34
(Corpus Christi: Thanksgiving for Eucharist)	
Friday	1 Corinthians 12: 1–13
Saturday	1 Corinthians 12: 14–31

Week beginning the first Sunday after Trinity

Monday	1 Corinthians 13
Tuesday	1 Corinthians 14: 1–12
Wednesday	1 Corinthians 14: 13–25

Thursday	1 Corinthians 14: 26–40
Friday	1 Thessalonians 5: 12–28
Saturday	Acts 2: 14–21

Week beginning the Second Sunday after Trinity

Monday	Acts 2: 22–4, 32–6
Tuesday	Acts 2: 37–47
Wednesday	Acts 3: 1–10
Thursday	Acts 3: 11–16
Friday	Acts 3: 17–26
Saturday	Acts 4: 1–12

Week beginning the Third Sunday after Trinity

Monday	Acts 4: 13–22
Tuesday	Acts 4: 23–31
Wednesday	Acts 4: 32–7
Thursday	Acts 5: 1–16
Friday	Acts 5: 17–32
Saturday	Acts 5: 33–42

ORDINARY TIME 2

Easter Day could fall on any day between 22 March and 25 April. Unless Easter is very late, you are unlikely to reach the end of the readings in this section.

Week beginning the Fourth Sunday after Trinity

Monday	Acts 6: 1–7
Tuesday	Acts 6: 8–15
Wednesday	Acts 7: 1–8, 51–60
Thursday	Acts 8: 1–8
Friday	Acts 8: 9–25
Saturday	Acts 8: 26–40

Suggested Bible Readings

Week beginning the Fifth Sunday after Trinity
Monday	Acts 9: 1–19a
Tuesday	Acts 9: 19b–30
Wednesday	Acts 9: 31–43
Thursday	**Acts 11: 1–18**
Friday	Acts 12: 1–11
Saturday	Acts 12: 12–25

Week beginning the Sixth Sunday after Trinity
Monday	Acts 13: 1–12
Tuesday	Acts 14: 1–20
Wednesday	Acts 15: 1–21
Thursday	Acts 15: 22–41
Friday	Acts 17: 16–34
Saturday	Acts 19: 1–22

Week beginning the Seventh Sunday after Trinity
Monday	Acts 19: 23–41
Tuesday	Acts 27: 1–26
Wednesday	Acts 27: 27–44
Thursday	Acts 28: 1–16
Friday	Acts 28: 17–31
Saturday	Mark 1: 1–13

Week beginning the Eighth Sunday after Trinity
Monday	Mark 1: 14–31
Tuesday	Mark 1: 32–45
Wednesday	Mark 2: 1–14
Thursday	Mark 2: 15–28
Friday	Mark 3: 1–12
Saturday	Mark 3: 13–35

Week beginning the Ninth Sunday after Trinity
Monday	Mark 4: 1–20
Tuesday	Mark 4: 21–34

Suggested Bible Readings

Wednesday	Mark 4: 35–41
Thursday	Mark 5: 1–20
Friday	Mark 5: 21–43
Saturday	Mark 6: 1–13

Week beginning the Tenth Sunday after Trinity

Monday	Mark 6: 14–29
Tuesday	Mark 6: 30–44
Wednesday	Mark 6: 45–56
Thursday	Mark 7: 1–23
Friday	Mark 7: 24–37
Saturday	Mark 8: 27–38

Week beginning the Eleventh Sunday after Trinity

Monday	Mark 9: 1–13
Tuesday	Mark 9: 14–32
Wednesday	Mark 9: 33–50
Thursday	Mark 10: 1–16
Friday	Mark 10: 17–31
Saturday	Mark 10: 32–45

Week beginning the Twelfth Sunday after Trinity

Monday	Mark 10: 46–52
Tuesday	Matthew 4: 1–11
Wednesday	Matthew 5: 1–12
Thursday	Matthew 5: 17–30
Friday	Matthew 5: 31–48
Saturday	Matthew 6: 1–15

Week beginning the Thirteenth Sunday after Trinity

Monday	Matthew 6: 16–24
Tuesday	**Matthew 6: 25–34**
Wednesday	Matthew 7: 1–14
Thursday	Matthew 7: 15–29
Friday	Matthew 18: 15–22

Suggested Bible Readings

Saturday   Matthew 18: 23–35

Week beginning the Fourteenth Sunday after Trinity
Monday   Matthew 25: 14–30
Tuesday   Matthew 25: 31–46
Wednesday   Luke 4: 14–30
Thursday   Luke 7: 1–17
Friday   Luke 7: 18–35
Saturday   Luke 7: 36–50

Week beginning the Fifteenth Sunday after Trinity
Monday   Luke 10: 25–37
Tuesday   Luke 10: 38–42
Wednesday   Luke 13: 31–5
Thursday   Luke 14: 7–14
Friday   Luke 14: 15–24
Saturday   Luke 14: 25–35

Week beginning the Sixteenth Sunday after Trinity
Monday   Luke 15: 1–10
Tuesday   Luke 15: 11–32
Wednesday   Luke 16: 1–15
Thursday   Luke 16: 19–31
Friday   Luke 17: 5–19
Saturday   Luke 17: 20–37

Week beginning the Seventeenth Sunday after Trinity
Monday   Luke 18: 1–8
Tuesday   Luke 18: 9–14
Wednesday   Luke 19: 1–10
Thursday   John 3: 1–15
Friday   John 3: 16–21
Saturday   John 3: 22–36

Suggested Bible Readings

Week beginning the Eighteenth Sunday after Trinity

Monday	John 4: 1–14
Tuesday	John 4: 15–30
Wednesday	John 4: 31–42
Thursday	John 6: 35–51
Friday	John 7: 37–52
Saturday	John 7: 53–8: 11

Week beginning the Nineteenth Sunday after Trinity
*All Saints' Day, 1 November, can fall on any day from now on;
move straight to* **All Saints' Tide** *on that day.*

	Year 1	Year 2
Monday	1 Samuel 3	2 Kings 17: 1–18
Tuesday	1 Samuel 9: 1–10, 14–27	2 Kings 18: 1–8, 13–18
Wednesday	1 Samuel 10: 1–16	2 Kings 18: 19–37
Thursday	1 Samuel 15: 10–11 and 16: 1–13	2 Kings 19: 1–21, 35–7
Friday	1 Samuel 16: 14–23	2 Kings 24: 8–17
Saturday	1 Samuel 17: 1–40	2 Kings 25: 8–12, 27–30

Week beginning the Twentieth Sunday after Trinity

Monday	1 Samuel 17: 41–58	Nehemiah 1
Tuesday	1 Samuel 18: 1–16, 28–30	Nehemiah 2
Wednesday	1 Samuel 19	Nehemiah 4*
Thursday	1 Samuel 31	Nehemiah 6: 15–7: 5a
Friday	2 Samuel 1: 17–27	Nehemiah 8: 1–12
Saturday	2 Samuel 5: 1–12	Nehemiah 12: 27–30, 44–7

** The passage beginning, 'When Sanballat . . .'. In some versions
this begins at 3: 33.*

Suggested Bible Readings

Week beginning the Twenty-first Sunday after Trinity

	Year 1	Year 2
Monday	2 Samuel 6	Job 1
Tuesday	2 Samuel 7: 1–17	Job 2
Wednesday	1 Kings 2: 1–4, 10–12; and 3: 1–4	Job 3
Thursday	1 Kings 3: 5–28	Job 15: 1–20
Friday	1 Kings 4: 20–34	Job 19
Saturday	1 Kings 7: 51–8: 21; 10: 23–5	Job 38: 1–21

Week beginning the Twenty-second Sunday after Trinity

	Year 1	Year 2
Monday	1 Peter 1: 1–12	Job 40: 3–5 and 42: 1–17
Tuesday	1 Peter 2: 1–10	James 1: 1–11
Wednesday	1 Peter 3: 13–22	James 1: 19–27
Thursday	1 Peter 4: 12–19	James 2: 14–26
Friday	1 Peter 5	James 3: 1–12
Saturday	2 Peter 1	James 5: 13–20

ALL SAINTS' TIDE

1 November *(All Saints' Day)*	**Revelation 7: 9–12**
2 November	Revelation 7: 13–17
3 November	**Hebrews 12: 1–2**
4 November	Jeremiah 1: 4–12
5 November	Jeremiah 2: 1–13
6 November	Jeremiah 3: 6–18
7 November	*a gap for whenever Sunday falls this week*

Suggested Bible Readings

	Year 1	Year 2
8 November	Isaiah 65: 17–25	Jeremiah 4: 19–31
9 November	Isaiah 66: 10–16	Jeremiah 7: 1–7, 21–6
10 November	Hosea 1: 2–3	Jeremiah 17: 5–18
	2: 2–13	
11 November	Hosea 2: 14–20	Jeremiah 18: 1–11
12 November	Hosea 5: 15–6: 6	Jeremiah 20: 7–18
13 November	Hosea 11: 1–9	Jeremiah 23: 1–8
14 November	*a gap for whenever Sunday falls this week*	
15 November	Hosea 14: 2–9	Jeremiah 24
16 November	Amos 5: 1–13	Jeremiah 29: 1–14
17 November	Amos 5: 14–24	Jeremiah 30: 1–17
18 November	Zechariah 2: 1–13	Jeremiah 30: 18–24
19 November	Zechariah 8: 1–17	Jeremiah 31: 1–9, 31–4

	Years 1 and 2
20 November	Revelation 1: 1–8
21 November	*a gap for whenever Sunday falls this week*
22 November	Revelation 1: 9–20
23 November	Revelation 4
24 November	Revelation 5: 1–10
25 November	Revelation 5: 11–14
26 November	Revelation 7: 13–17

*Move on to the season of **Advent** on Advent Sunday, which may fall on any day between 27 November and 3 December*

27 November	Revelation 12
28 November	Revelation 20: 1–6
29 November	Revelation 21: 1–8
30 November	Revelation 21: 9–27

Suggested Bible Readings

1 December   Revelation 22: 1–7
2 December   Revelation 22: 8–21
3 December   *a gap for whenever Sunday falls this week*

Appendix A

Prayers for Saints' Days

These prayers can be used instead of the set prayer at the end of the Short Orders of Daily Prayer.

25 January – Conversion of St Paul (St Paul is also remembered in the RC Church on 29 June)
Convert us,
Jesus the persecuted,
as you converted Paul
and sent him as apostle to the world.
May our love, our prayers, our suffering
carry your gospel at whatever cost
to all who wait to hear it.

A New Zealand Prayer Book

2 February – Presentation of Jesus in the Temple (or Candlemas)
Lord we praise you for the quiet strength of Joseph,
    the prophetic insight of Simeon,
    the self-dedication of Anna,
    and the courage of Mary
    as she faced the truth
    that a sword would pierce her heart.
make us bearers of your light which lightens the world,
and help us, like Simeon, to live for you and depart in
  peace.

19 March – St Joseph

Father,
you entrusted our Saviour to the care of Saint Joseph.
   By the help of his prayers
may your church continue to serve its Lord, Jesus Christ,
who lives and reigns with you and the Holy Spirit,
one God, for ever and ever. Amen

The Roman Missal

25 March – The Annunciation of Our Lord

God we thank you
that you made yourself known
to someone without power, wealth or status;
and we praise you
for the courage of Mary,
this young woman from Galilee,
whose Yes to the shame and shock
of bearing your Son
let loose the unstoppable power of love
which changed the world.

25 April – St Mark

We give thanks, O God, for your servant John Mark:
for the grace by which he triumphed over early failure,
and for the inspiration by which he penned the story of
the strong Son of God.

Teach us through his life and writings the secret of
victorious living, and deepen our faith in your redeeming love and power, made known to us in Jesus Christ
our Lord.

Frank Colquhoun

Prayers for Saints' Days

8 May – Julian of Norwich

Gentle God, ground of our beseeching,
you enfold us in goodness
and wrap us tenderly as in a garment;
we praise you for Julian
and her knowledge of your love.
God our Father, our Mother, our Spouse,
let love be our meaning,
as it is yours,
and make us your bliss, your honour and your crown,
in the love with which you loved us
before we were born.

31 May – The Visit of the Blessed Virgin Mary to Elizabeth

Lord Jesus, grant us the double joy of Mary and
Elizabeth: the joy of carrying you in our hearts, and the
joy of recognizing you in the hearts of others, that out
of joy may come praise, telling out the greatness of God
our Saviour.

Susan Williams

11 June – St Barnabas

Free us, Lord, from a spirit of cynicism
or the desire to condemn,
and make us, like Barnabas,
generous in our judgements,
bold in trusting others,
and loyal to our friends.
Fill us with your Spirit of peace,
that we may be a source of support and comfort
to all in need;
for your love's sake.

Prayers for Saints' Days

24 June – Birth of St John the Baptist

Who was this man, Lord,
wild and unkempt,
ascetic and outspoken?
Jesus, you knew him and loved him
and grieved at his death.
Unblock our ears now
to the voice of your cousin:
refine our wills in your winnowing wind,
and help us, like John,
to bear witness to you,
for the coming of your kingdom
and the fire of your love.

29 June – St Peter (RC: St Peter and St Paul))

God of grace,
your Church is built on Peter's faith;
grant that we, like him, forgiven and restored,
may overcome our weakness
and serve you without wavering,
now and for ever.

A New Zealand Prayer Book

3 July – St Thomas

Forgive us, Lord,
when we want proofs of our faith
and demand absolute certainty
before we will commit ourselves to you.
Strengthen our trust in you,
so that we, who have not seen you,
may still believe,
and in believing may be blessed
with the fullness of joy,
now and always.

Cf. John 20: 26–9

Prayers for Saints' Days

11 July – St Benedict of Nursia
Almighty God,
by whose grace St. Benedict
kindled with the fire of your love,
became a burning and a shining light in the church;
inflame us with the same spirit
of discipline and love,
that we may walk before you
as children of light;
through Jesus Christ our Lord, Amen.

The Alternative Service Book, 1980

22 July – St Mary Magdalene
Sweet is your friendship, Saviour Christ;
Mary you accepted,
Mary you drew to the foot of the cross,
Mary you met in the garden;
grant us a like redemption
that we may be healed
and serve you in the power of your risen life.

A New Zealand Prayer Book

25 July – St James
O God, we remember today your apostle James, first
among the Twelve to suffer martyrdom for the name of
Jesus; and we pray that you will give to the leaders of
your church that spirit of self-denying service which is
the hallmark of true authority among your people;
through Jesus Christ our Lord.

The Book of Common Prayer *of the*
Episcopal Church, USA (adapted)

6 August – The Transfiguration of Our Lord
Christ our only true light,
before whose bright cloud
your friends fell to the ground:
we bow before your cross
that we may remember in our bodies
the dead who fell like shadows;
and that we may refuse to be prostrated
before the false brightness of any other light,
looking to your power alone
for hope of resurrection from the dead.

Janet Morley
6 August is also the day the nuclear bomb
was dropped on Hiroshima.

21 September – St Matthew
Lord, thank you
for loving Matthew enough
to believe in him
and call him
out of the chaos and corruption of tax-collecting
into life with you.
Open our eyes to see
that you believe in us too,
and give us grace to receive
the freedom you offer
when you say, 'Follow me.'

29 September – St Michael and All Angels
Blessèd Lord of angels and archangels,
we praise you for the brightness of your love.
Give your angels charge over us,
to guard us against the powers of evil.
May these beings of light

encircle and protect us,
so that we may serve you better
and never lose our vision of your heavenly glory.

Cf. Psalm 91: 11

4 October – St Francis

Lord Jesus Christ,
who when the world was growing cold,
to the inflaming of our hearts by the fire of your love
raised up blessèd Francis
bearing in his body the marks of your passion:
mercifully grant to us, your people, true penitence,
and grace to bear the Cross for love of you;
who live and reign with the Father and the Holy Spirit,
one God, now and for ever.

Celebrating Common Prayer (for the Stigmata of St Francis)

18 October – St Luke

Healing God,
we thank you for Luke,
the 'beloved physician',
and for his faithful recording
of the life of your Son
and the birth of the church.
Continue in us your work of healing:
may we never pass by on the other side,
but rather reach out to the poor and sick
and those on the margins,
in the love of Jesus our Lord.

Cf. Colossians 4: 14

Prayers for Saints' Days

1 November – All Saints

Lord, we thank you for your saints,
and ask for grace to follow them:
make us open like Mary your mother
and bold like Paul;
joyful like Francis,
and faithful like Clare.
Help us to reflect
Mary Magdalene's great love for you,
John the Evangelist's understanding of you,
and Peter's steadfast devotion to you;
 and when we feel we have failed you,
 remind us that all your saints
 knew they were sinners in need of your mercy;
 for your love's sake.

30 November – St Andrew

Almighty God,
who gave such grace to your apostle Saint Andrew
that he readily obeyed the call of your Son Jesus Christ
 and brought his brother with him:
call us by your holy word,
and give us grace to follow you without delay
 and to tell the good news of your kingdom;
through Jesus Christ your Son our Lord,
who is alive and reigns with you,
in the unity of the Holy Spirit,
one God, now and for ever.

The Christian Year, Calendar, Lectionary and Collects

26 December – St Stephen

For the courage of Stephen, I thank you;
for courage to stand up for what I believe, I ask you.
For the strength of all who died for you, I thank you;
for strength to stand firm when the crowd disagrees, I ask
  you.
Father of mercy, bless my efforts to love you,
and help me, in spite of my uncertainties,
  to hear your call,
  follow your way,
  and surrender my life into your hands.

27 December – St John the Evangelist

Shed upon your church, O Lord, the brightness of your
light, that we, being illumined by the teaching of your
apostle and evangelist John, may walk in the light of
your truth, and abide in you for ever; through Jesus
Christ our Lord.

The Book of Common Prayer *of the Episcopal
Church, USA (adapted)*

Appendix B

'Lectio Divina': Sacred Reading

This ancient approach to Scripture, which means, literally, 'divine' or 'sacred reading', goes back to the Desert Fathers and Mothers of fourth-century Egypt and was developed further by St Benedict in the sixth century. These teachers of prayer knew that the message of the Bible is not fully understood simply through study. We also have to allow it to touch our hearts, leading us into communion with God. So they devised this simple form of listening to the word, to help us not only to know *about* God, but to know God through experience. This pattern has been followed in a variety of forms ever since. The Latin names for the different stages are included here, as a reminder of our heritage and rootedness in the vibrant faith and practice of Christians in the past.

Reading *(Lectio)*: read the passage slowly and thoughtfully, perhaps twice. See if any word or phrase leaps out, or seems to be particularly apt for you today.

Meditation *(Meditatio)*: stay with those words and repeat them peacefully to yourself, letting them sink from your head into your heart. Continue to repeat the words for a while, either articulating them with your lips or just saying them in your mind. Allow the word or phrase to find its way to your inner being, 'as gently as a feather falling on a piece of cotton wool'.[1]

Verbal Response *(Oratio)*: talk to God in whatever way you want, in response to what has been offered to you.

Contemplation *(Contemplatio)*: move into quiet communion with God, resting in the divine presence, and gently coming back to those key words whenever your mind wanders.

Notes and Acknowledgements

The picture at the beginning of each season is by the late Sr Margaret Tournour RSCJ, © Society of the Sacred Heart.

Introduction

1. I owe this insight to Paula Gooder, *This Risen Existence*, Norwich: Canterbury Press, 2009, page 3.

Advent – A Short Order of Daily Prayer

The Great Os: *Western Rite (adapted by A.A.)* Originally in *The Book of a Thousand Prayers*, Grand Rapids, Michigan: Zondervan, 2002.

Prayer beginning, 'God of all hope and joy': this copyright material is taken from *A New Zealand Prayer Book – He Karakia Mihinare o Aotearoa* (1989) and is used with permission.

Advent – A Quiet Space

No. 2. 'Lord Jesus Christ, you came to a stable . . .': from *A Worship Anthology for Advent and Christmas*, ed. H. J. Richards, Bury St Edmunds: Kevin Mayhew Ltd, 1994, page 32.

No. 4. The idea of waiting on God in prayer 'as the parched earth looking upwards, waiting patiently for the rain to fall' comes from an address by Robert Llewelyn at a Taizé Service, printed in *Fairacres Chronicle*, Summer 1996, Oxford: SLG Press.

Notes and Acknowledgements

The paraphrase of Psalm 62: 1 comes from *By Stony Paths*, Jim Cotter, Sheffield: Cairns Publications, 1991.

Christmas – A Short Order of Daily Prayer

Prayer beginning, 'Son of God, Child of Mary . . .': this copyright material is taken from *A New Zealand Prayer Book – He Karakia Mihinare o Aotearoa (1989)* and is used with permission.

Prayer beginning, 'Jesus, Son of God . . .': originally in *The Book of a Thousand Prayers*, Grand Rapids, Michigan: Zondervan, 2002.

Christmas – A Quiet Space

No. 2. 'Jesus is the "enfleshment" . . .' by Kenneth Stevenson: *On the Receiving End*, London: Mowbray, a Cassell Imprint, 1996, page 4.

No. 3. Line drawing of the icon © Paul Judson.

Christmas – Night-Time Blessing

The copyright owner has not been traced. The prayer appears in *The Promise of His Glory*, © The Central Board of Finance of the Church of England, 1989.

Epiphany – A Short Order of Daily Prayer

The Nunc Dimittis (Song of Simeon): material from *Celebrating Common Prayer* (Mowbray), © The Society of St Francis 1992, is used with permission.

Prayer beginning, 'Lord Jesus, I offer you the gold . . .': originally in *The Book of a Thousand Prayers*, Grand Rapids, Michigan: Zondervan, 2002; slightly adapted (the original begins, 'Jesus, we offer you . . .').

Notes and Acknowledgements

Epiphany – A Quiet Space

No. 2. Excerpt from the sermon by Michael Stancliffe, *Wise Men's Faith*, from *Stars and Angels*, The Canterbury Press Norwich, 1997, page 39.

No. 3. Hymn: 'Why, impious Herod . . .': translated by Percy Dearmer, English Hymnal No. 38, A. R. Mowbray & Co., Ltd, 1933.

No. 4. Words by Evelyn Underhill from *The House of the Soul*, Methuen, 1926, page 146.

No. 5. Passage by Mother Jane Margaret CSMV, reproduced with permission from the Community of St Mary the Virgin.

No. 7. Line drawing of the icon © Paul Judson.

Epiphany – Night-Time Blessing

Reproduced by permission © Ruth Burgess.

Ordinary Time 1 – A Short Order of Daily Prayer

The Jubilate: material from *Celebrating Common Prayer* (Mowbray), © The Society of St Francis 1992, is used with permission.

Prayer beginning, 'O God of truth and mercy . . .' by Jim Cotter: *Through Desert Places*, page 89, Cairns Publications, 47, Firth Park Avenue, Sheffield S5 6HF.

Ordinary Time 1 – A Quiet Space

No. 2. 'You want to seek God . . .': from *Rule for a New Brother*, by the Brakkenstein Community of Blessed Sacrament Fathers, Holland; London: Darton, Longman and Todd Ltd, 1973, pages 1–2.

Notes and Acknowledgements

Lent – A Short Order of Daily Prayer

'Saviour of the World' by Henry Allon; quoted in *Celebrating Common Prayer* as Canticle No. 67. Material from *Celebrating Common Prayer* (Mowbray), © The Society of St Francis 1992, is used with permission.

Prayer beginning, 'Almighty and everlasting God, you despise nothing . . .': *Scottish Liturgy 1982*, © 1989 General Synod of the Scottish Episcopal Church.

Prayer beginning, 'Lord, in these days of mercy . . .': originally in *The Book of a Thousand Prayers*, Grand Rapids, Michigan: Zondervan, 2002.

Lent – A Quiet Space

No. 2. 'Prayer springs from . . .': Maria Boulding, from *Marked for Life*, London: SPCK Triangle, 1985, page 85.

No. 3. Prayer beginning, 'Merciful God . . .': *The Pattern of our Days*, ed. Kathy Galloway © Wild Goose Publications/The Iona Community, Glasgow: 1996. Slightly adapted.

Quotations from Julian of Norwich's *Revelations of the Divine Love*: from the translation by Fr. John-Julian OJN, *A Lesson of Love*, Chapters 39 and 40, London: Darton, Longman and Todd Ltd, 1988.

No. 4. Quotation from Austin Farrar: *Lord I Believe*, London: Faith Press, 1958, page 88.

No. 6. Passage by Bonhoeffer in *The Cost of Discipleship*, London: SCM Press Ltd, 1959 edition.

Holy Week – A Short Order of Daily Prayer

'Now my tongue the mystery telling . . .': translated by J. M. Neale (1818–66), E. Caswall (1814–78) and others. *Hymns Ancient & Modern New Standard*, The Canterbury Press, Norwich, 1984, No. 252.

Notes and Acknowledgements

Prayer beginning, 'Jesus, Lord of the Cross . . .': originally in *The Book of a Thousand Prayers*, Grand Rapids, Michigan: Zondervan, 2002.

Holy Week – A Quiet Space

No. 2. 'There was a scaffold . . .' by Martin Niemöller, in *Against Torture*, quoted in *Liturgy of Life*, ed. Donald Hilton, Birmingham: NCEC, 1991.

No. 4. 'Let this cup . . .' by Donald Nicholl, in *Holiness*, London: Darton, Longman and Todd Ltd, 1981, page 154.

'United with us in being . . .' by Olivier Clément, in *The Roots of Christian Mysticism*, London: New City, 1993, page 44.

Prayer beginning, 'Christ, pouring yourself out . . .': originally in *The Book of a Thousand Prayers*, Grand Rapids, Michigan: Zondervan, 2002, slightly adapted. (The original began, 'O Christ, pouring . . .'.)

Line drawing of the chalice © Paul Judson.

Easter – A Short Order of Daily Prayer

Prayer beginning, 'Almighty Father, who in your great mercy . . .': *The Christian Year: Calendar, Lectionary and Collects*, London: Church House Publishing, 1997, © The Central Board of Finance of the Church of England.

Prayer beginning, 'Love of Jesus, fill me . . .' is inspired by the traditional invocation of Christ, the 'Anima Christi'.

Easter – A Quiet Space

No. 3. Line drawing of the icon © Paul Judson.

Easter – Night-Time Blessing

'Friday Blessing' from *Prayer at Night's Approaching*, page 117. Cairns Publications, 47, Firth Park Avenue, Sheffield S5 6HF.

Notes and Acknowledgements

Ascension – A Short Order of Daily Prayer

Prayer beginning, 'Ascended Christ, present at all times . . .': originally in *The Book of a Thousand Prayers,* Grand Rapids, Michigan: Zondervan, 2002, adapted. (The original began, 'Ascended Christ, we worship you . . .'.)

Prayer beginning, 'Eternal God, by raising Jesus . . .': this copyright material is taken from *A New Zealand Prayer Book – He Karakia Mihinare o Aotearoa (1989)* and is used with permission.

Ascension – A Quiet Space

No. 2. Quotation by Austin Farrar: *The Crown of the Year: Weekly Paragraphs for the Holy Sacrament,* London: Dacre Press, 1953, page 34.

Quotation by Teilhard de Chardin: *La Messe du Monde,* William Collins Sons & Co. Ltd, London, and Harper & Brothers, New York, Section 12.

No. 3. 'What Jesus did . . .' by John Bowker: *The Church Times* 1991 (exact date unknown).

Pentecost – A Short Order of Daily Prayer

Prayer beginning, 'Father of light . . .': *The Sunday Missal,* Second Collect for the Mass during the day on Pentecost Sunday, page 282. Excerpts from the English translation of *The Roman Missal,* (c) 1973, International Committee on English in the Liturgy, Inc. All rights reserved.

Prayer beginning, 'Almighty and all-loving God . . .': originally in *The Book of a Thousand Prayers,* Grand Rapids, Michigan: Zondervan, 2002, slightly adapted.

Notes and Acknowledgements

Pentecost – A Quiet Space

No. 3. 'Whenever we pray as Christians . . .' by Paul Bradshaw, *Two Ways of Praying*, London: SPCK, 1995, page 64.

'Prayer is the energy . . .' by André Louf, *Teach us to Pray*, London: Darton, Longman and Todd Ltd., 1974, page 86.

No. 4. 'Holy Spirit, fire of love . . .'. This prayer comes originally from Meditation 12, *Wait and Trust*, Guildford: Eagle, an imprint of Inter Publishing Service (IPS) Ltd, 1997.

No. 5. Three quotations by Austin Farrar, 'His action is like the rising water . . .': *Saving Belief*, London: Hodder & Stoughton 1964, page 125.

'How does the Spirit of Christ . . .': *The End of Man*, ed. Charles C. Conti. London: SPCK, 1973, page 65.

'When we allow the love . . .': *The Crown of the Year: Weekly Paragraphs for the Holy Sacrament*. London: Dacre Press 1953, page 41.

No. 6. '*The Father*: God's being . . .' by Rowan Williams, *Open to Judgement*, London: Darton, Longman and Todd Ltd, 1994, page 24.

'Living Love . . .': © Brian A. Wren, 3, Union St, Apt. 2, Topsham, ME 04086, USA. Used by permission.

No. 7. Line drawing of the icon © Paul Judson.

Pentecost – Night-Time Blessing

Worship in an Indian Context, ed. Eric J. Lott, © 1986 United Theological College, Bangalore.

Ordinary Time 2 – A Short Order of Daily Prayer

Psalm prayer at the end of Psalm 25, based on an original (No. 901) in *The Book of a Thousand Prayers*, Grand Rapids, Michigan: Zondervan, 2002.

Notes and Acknowledgements

Verses from the Benedicite: These come originally from The Song of the Three Jews (verses 35–66), an addition to the Book of Daniel now found in the Apocrypha; written in Aramaic, *c*. 130 BC).

Prayer beginning 'Jesus, Son of God, let your love . . .': *Prayers for the People,* ed. Michael Perry, London: HarperCollins, 1992.

Ordinary Time 2 – A Quiet Space

No. 2. 'Here I am, Lord. I cannot fathom or hold you . . .': slightly adapted from an original prayer in *The Book of a Thousand Prayers,* Grand Rapids, Michigan: Zondervan, 2002 (where it began: 'Lord, I cannot . . .).

No. 4. Line drawing of the icon © Paul Judson.

Prayer beginning, 'Heaven and earth, O Lord . . .': material from *Celebrating Common Prayer* (Mowbray), © The Society of St Francis 1992, is used with permission.

No. 5. 'The hardest thing . . .' by Maria Boulding: *Marked for Life,* London: SPCK Triangle, 1985.

No. 7. 'It is not . . .' from *The Cloud of Unknowing*, ed. William Johnston, Garden City, NY: Doubleday Image Books, 1973.

'My Lord God, I have no idea where I am going . . .': from the anthology *Pax Christi,* Benet Press, 6601 East Lake Road, Erie, PA 16511, USA. Quoted by Esther de Waal in *A Seven Day Journey with Thomas Merton,* Guildford: Eagle, 1992.

No. 9. Talk by Jean Vanier: BBC2, November 1993.

Prayer beginning, 'God our lover . . .' by Janet Morley: *All Desires Known,* London: SPCK, 1992.

Ordinary Time 2 – Night-Time Blessing

Originally in *The Book of a Thousand Prayers,* Grand Rapids, Michigan: Zondervan, 2002.

Notes and Acknowledgements

All Saints' Tide – A Short Order of Daily Prayer

Verses from the Te Deum: material from *Celebrating Common Prayer* (Mowbray), © The Society of St Francis 1992, is used with permission.

Prayer beginning, 'We praise and thank you, Holy Spirit of God . . .': this copyright material is taken from *A New Zealand Prayer Book – He Karakia Mihinare o Aotearoa (1989)* and is used with permission.

All Saints' Tide – A Quiet Space

No. 2. Maggie Ross, *The Fire of Your Life*, The Lamp Press, Basingstoke: Marshall Pickering, 1988, pages 87–8.

No. 3. 'We thank thee . . .': verses 2 and 3 from the hymn 'The day thou gavest, Lord, is ended', *Hymns Ancient & Modern New Standard*, The Canterbury Press, Norwich, 1984, No. 16.

All Saints' Tide – Night-Time Blessing

Enriching the Christian Year, ed. Michael Perham, London: SPCK, 1993.

Appendix A – Prayers for Saints' Days

Conversion of St Paul: this copyright material is taken from *A New Zealand Prayer Book – He Karakia Mihinare o Aotearoa (1989)* and is used with permission.

Presentation of Jesus: originally in *The Book of a Thousand Prayers*, Grand Rapids, Michigan: Zondervan, 2002.

St Joseph: excerpts from the English translation of *The Roman Missal*, (c) 1973, International Committee on English in the Liturgy, Inc. All rights reserved.

The Annunciation: originally in *The Book of a Thousand Prayers*, Grand Rapids, Michigan: Zondervan, 2002.

Notes and Acknowledgements

St Mark: *Contemporary Parish Prayers* (1975), ed. Frank Colquhoun, London: Hodder & Stoughton Ltd.

Julian of Norwich: originally in *The Book of a Thousand Prayers*, Grand Rapids, Michigan: Zondervan, 2002.

The Visit of the BVM to Elizabeth: *Lord of Our World* (1973), Falcon Press. Falcon Books were published by CPAS, who are now at Athena Drive, Tachbrook Park, Warwick, CV34 6NG.

St Barnabas: originally in *The Book of a Thousand Prayers*, Grand Rapids, Michigan: Zondervan, 2002.

Birth of St John the Baptist: originally in *The Book of a Thousand Prayers*, Grand Rapids, Michigan: Zondervan, 2002.

St Peter: this copyright material is taken from *A New Zealand Prayer Book – He Karakia Mihinare o Aotearoa* (1989) and is used with permission.

St Thomas: originally in *The Book of a Thousand Prayers*, Grand Rapids, Michigan: Zondervan, 2002.

St Benedict of Nursia: *The Alternative Service Book 1980*, © The Central Board of Finance of the Church of England.

St Mary Magdalene: this copyright material is taken from *A New Zealand Prayer Book – He Karakia Mihinare o Aotearoa* (1989) and is used with permission.

St James: in the public domain, so no copyright permission necessary. Format: The Church Hymnal Corporation, New York, USA.

The Transfiguration: *All Desires Known*, London: SPCK, 1992.

St Matthew: originally in *The Book of a Thousand Prayers*, Grand Rapids, Michigan: Zondervan, 2002.

St Michael and All Angels: originally in *The Book of a Thousand Prayers*, Grand Rapids, Michigan: Zondervan, 2002.

St Francis: material from *Celebrating Common Prayer* (Mowbray), © The Society of St Francis 1992, is used with permission.

Notes and Acknowledgements

St Luke: originally in *The Book of a Thousand Prayers*, Grand Rapids, Michigan: Zondervan, 2002.

All Saints: originally in *The Book of a Thousand Prayers*, Grand Rapids, Michigan: Zondervan, 2002.

St Andrew: *The Christian Year: Calendar, Lectionary and Collects*, London: Church House Publishing, 1997, © The Central Board of Finance of the Church of England.

St Stephen: originally in *The Book of a Thousand Prayers*, Grand Rapids, Michigan: Zondervan, 2002.

St John the Evangelist: in the public domain, so no copyright permission necessary. Format: The Church Hymnal Corporation, New York, USA.

Appendix B – 'Lectio Divina'

1. This is an Anglicized version of the phrase 'laying a feather on a piece of absorbent cotton' in *Open Mind, Open Heart* by Thomas Keating, New York: Continuum, 1996, page 110.